Infinite Animation
The Life and Work
of Adam Beckett

The Focus Animation Series aims to provide unique, accessible content that may not otherwise be published. We allow researchers, academics, and professionals the ability to quickly publish high-impact, current literature in the field of animation for a global audience.

This series is a fine complement to the existing, robust animation titles available through CRC Press/Focal Press.

Series Editor Giannalberto Bendazzi, currently an independent scholar, is a former visiting professor of history of animation at the Nanyang Technological University in Singapore and a former professor at the Università degli Studi di Milano. We welcome any submissions to help grow the wonderful content that we are striving to provide to the animation community: giannalbertobendazzi@gmail.com.

Published:

Giannalberto Bendazzi; *Twice the First: Quirino Cristiani and the Animated Feature Film*

Maria Roberta Novielli; *Floating Worlds: A Short History of Japanese Animation*

Cinzia Bottini; *Redesigning Animation: United Productions of America*

Forthcoming:

Lina X. Aguirre; *Experimental Animation in Contemporary Latin America*

Marco Bellano; *Václav Trojan: Music Composition in Czech Animated Films*

Rolf Giesen; *Puppetry, Puppet Animation and the Digital Age*

Infinite Animation
The Life and Work
of Adam Beckett

Pamela Taylor Turner

CRC Press
Taylor & Francis Group
Boca Raton London New York

CRC Press is an imprint of the
Taylor & Francis Group, an **informa** business

CRC Press
Taylor & Francis Group
6000 Broken Sound Parkway NW, Suite 300
Boca Raton, FL 33487-2742

© 2019 by Taylor & Francis Group, LLC
CRC Press is an imprint of Taylor & Francis Group, an Informa business

No claim to original U.S. Government works

Printed on acid-free paper

International Standard Book Number-13: 978-0-8153-8200-3 (Hardback)

Library of Congress Cataloging-in-Publication Data

Names: Turner, Pamela Taylor, author.
Title: Infinite animation : the life and work of Adam Beckett / Pamela Taylor Turner.
Description: Boca Raton, FL : CRC Press, Taylor & Francis Group, 2019. | Includes bibliographical references.
Identifiers: LCCN 2018043551 | ISBN 9780815382003 (hardback : alk. paper)
Subjects: LCSH: Beckett, Adam, 1950-1979. | Animators--United States--Biography. | Beckett, Adam, 1950-1979--Criticism and interpretation.
Classification: LCC NC1766.U52 B4338 2019 | DDC 741.5/8092 [B] --dc23
LC record available at https://lccn.loc.gov/2018043551

Visit the Taylor & Francis Web site at
http://www.taylorandfrancis.com

and the CRC Press Web site at
http://www.crcpress.com

This manuscript is dedicated to my students, past and present.

Contents

Acknowledgments

A<small>DAM</small> B<small>ECKETT'S</small> <small>LIFE AND</small> work touched many people, and it has been my privilege to meet many of them and an honor to be trusted with their stories, insight, and knowledge. I am truly grateful. I will attempt to acknowledge everyone; please pardon me for any oversights.

Heartfelt thanks goes to the iotaCenter for the support and commitment to Adam's work through the establishment of The Adam Beckett Project. A special thanks goes to its founding director, and my dear friend, Larry Cuba, who introduced me to Adam's animations and encouraged me along the way.

My deep gratitude goes to Adam's family for their invaluable support and generosity in sharing Adam's story and his art: his mother, the late Julie Gilliam; his sister Deirdre Beckett; and his half-brother, Evan Gallas. I am especially thankful to Evan for graciously facilitating my access to Adam's drawings and artifacts. I sincerely thank you all for trusting me with this project.

Appreciation and thanks goes to Mark Toscano at the Academy Film Archive for his dedication to the Beckett films. His expertise and commitment made Adam's work new again. Thanks also goes to the iotaCenter interns who worked closely with Mark.

A special thanks to close friends of Adam: David and Diana Wilson, of the Museum of Jurassic Technology in Culver City, who shared such lovely memories; Dave Berry, Adam's colleague, close friend, and neighbor; Kathy Rose, who made critical contributions that no one else could have made; and Chris Casady, who shared stories, insight, audio, and photographs. Their enthusiasm, admiration, and love for Adam assured me that the project I had chosen—or that had chosen me—was a worthy expedition.

Many of his friends and colleagues contributed facts and stories that helped to build a more rounded picture of Adam as a person, shed light on his work, and made his lasting impact obvious. These include the late Brian Bailey, Richard "Dr" Baily, Tom Barron, Beth Block, Larry Cuba, Sky David, Loring Doyle, Roberta Friedman, Jeff Jurich, Daina Krumins, Gar LaSalle, George Lockwood, Rob Luttrell, Sara Petty, Tom Schiller, Michael Scroggins, Jon Seay, Ric Stafford, Byron Werner, and Z'ev. It was Casady and Cuba, whose repeated reference to Adam in the context of visual music first made me aware of his influence and the need for this project.

Mark Whitney's thoughtful understanding and appreciation of Adam's authenticity, even as a young teenager, were critical in creating a full story of this artist. Adam's earliest friends John and Victoria Koenig were an incredible resource, as they knew him for his entire life. Carl Stone remembers the Beckett siblings from high school and later contributed the sound score to Adam's *Evolution of the Red Star*. His memories and insight into Adam's process were invaluable.

Barry Schrader provided invaluable insight into the making of Beckett's *Heavy-Light* and Adam's perspective at that time. His knowledge of the history of the music program at CalArts was extremely helpful.

A special thanks goes to Pat O'Neill, who introduced Adam to the optical printer at CalArts and worked alongside him for a few years; many thanks to him for sharing his memories and critical perspective.

Libby Chaney helped to illuminate the art circle that emanated from Cathy Heerman and the Junior Art Center at Barnsdall, as well as helped to decode the "Dear Libby" drawing. Christine Bleackley offered great insight into aspects of Adam's personal life during and after his work on *Star Wars*.

A special thank you to James Gore; his contribution to Adam's life and life story is essential.

Shalom Gorewitz and Bill Brand shared important perspectives from their time at Antioch College, with Shalom being able to reflect on Adam's presence at CalArts as well. Alison Knowles provided invaluable insight into the role of Fluxus on the new campus and the program that was being fostered at CalArts.

There are numerous colleagues and peers from the visual effects industry who witnessed the re-ignition of the visual effects industry and shared insight into Adam's contributions and how he fit into that world. These include Dave Berry, Robert Blalock, Deena Burkett, Chris Casady, Richard Edlund, Jonathan Erland, Peter Kuran, Dennis Muren, Jon Seay, Jerome Seven, Richard W. Taylor, and Diana Wilson.

David Lebrun first alerted me to Adam's time with the Hog Farm. Jean Nichols and Dorgie Bonds were invaluable in painting a picture of life with the Farm and also the spirit of the late 1960s and early 1970s.

Jim Trainor was helpful, and generous, in sharing a letter that he received from Adam in May of 1978.

I would also like to thank John Hanhardt for his encouragement and his insight into Adam's films and for the information he shared generously regarding the New American Filmmakers program.

A special thanks goes to Virginia Commonwealth University's School of the Arts.

To my copy-editor Kathy Jones, sincere thanks for your keen eyes and helpful suggestions.

A huge debt of gratitude is owed to my friends and family, including my four-legged crew, for their unfailing support, and for their patience as I worked long hours away from them.

CHAPTER 1

Auspicious Beginnings

The Young Artist in 1950s Los Angeles and Abroad

A DAM KEMPER BECKETT HAS been described as a shooting star, brilliantly appearing and evoking wonder, and then vanishing, leaving a fading trail of animation art to mark his passing. Where his path would have taken him—if it had continued—is anybody's guess, especially as his art was developing at the cusp of change ushered in by computer graphics and video image processing. Retracing his steps provides a critical look at his work and its prominent place in the fertile independent animation culture that emerged in the United States during the 1970s.

Adam's animation has kinship with West Coast cinema of the time period, through its focus on abstraction and transcendence. He used metamorphosis (a technique native to straight-ahead drawn animation) and image processing, with an eye toward transformation, not only of forms but also of the viewer, through the filmic experience. As curator John Hanhardt recalls Adam's work, "... his vigorous treatment of the drawing and spatial configurations that he would create were powerfully inventive and compelling."[1] His work conveyed humor, not unlike the irreverent play of Nam June Paik that Adam witnessed firsthand at the California Institute of the Arts. There, he also became well-versed in the prophetic and timely vision of Gene Youngblood's expanded cinema, which provides a valuable key in examining the "synaesthetic cinema" that Adam created.

Adam's work was heralded in the 1970s, as a new era of independent animation took hold in the United States. The optimism and support faded in the 1980s, owing to the changes in distribution and funding. The gap between video and film versus animation widened. Even abstract, transcendental animated films were largely ignored by film scholars, galleries, and museums, relegated to a less serious cinematic form. The broader practice and experience of moving-image media have been acknowledged and a more democratic approach in critical thinking has been applied only in the twentieth century; expanded cinema could no longer be ignored. With this broadened mediascape, Adam's work can be revisited and examined as a practice absorbing and reflecting the change in culture and in cinema.

Adam Beckett was born on February 1, 1950, in Los Angeles, the epicenter of cinema on the West Coast. It was also a city undergoing a postwar boom in population and development. Adam was the first child of creative, intellectual parents from affluent backgrounds; he spent his earliest years in a home in Bel-Air, surrounded by art. His father was William Sutherland Beckett, a promising young architect, and his mother, Julianne (Julie) Kemper Beckett, was from the prominent Midwestern Kemper banking family.

Both parents had come to Los Angeles from Kansas City, Missouri. Julie Beckett had graduated from Bennington, a fairly new and somewhat experimental college in Vermont. This influence would be apparent in the alternative education that she later insisted on for her children. William Beckett received his degree in architecture from Yale University and moved to Los Angeles in 1944, during World War II, to work at Douglas Aircraft.

According to Adam's sister, Deirdre Beckett, their parents did not know each other until meeting in Los Angeles, at Ciro's, mingling with the young elite.[2] They got married in 1948 in Kansas City. By 1950, William Sutherland Beckett had set up his own architectural firm and opened his office at 9026 Melrose; the remodeling of that space won him the highly esteemed American Institute of Architects (AIA) award in 1952. This office was next to the Stage Society Theater, which, in 1973, became Theatre Vanguard, where Adam would have his animations screened alongside other avant-garde films.

Adam's parents were active in the Los Angeles arts community and social scene. His father was elected to the Los Angeles Arts Commission in 1951, and his mother amassed a collection over the years. They were in the *Los Angeles Times* society pages during the winter holidays of 1953. "In the West Side social orbit chatter goes on about parties to come and parties gone by. Being received today are clever invitations from the William S. Becketts of Bel-Air for cocktails and supper Saturday afternoon after 4 p.m."[3] By then, the 3-year-old Adam had two younger siblings: Morgan, born in September 1951, and Deirdre, born in August 1952.

The senior Beckett made his mark in architecture with modern, clean designs that appeared in magazines such as *Arts and Architecture* and *Architectural Forum*. The remodel of a French Regency house in Bel-Air, purchased as a home for his growing family, was covered in detail in the May 1952 issue of *House and Home*.[4] The house was updated to have a modern aesthetic, with a simplified façade in the back, glass openings that allowed better access to the outdoor area, and a new wing housing a 600-square-foot master bedroom.

This auspicious setting for Adam's earliest years would soon change. In March 1954, the Becketts purchased another home, on Summit Drive in Beverly Hills. According to the *Los Angeles Times*, this had been the estate of Stanley McCormick, the son of Cyrus McCormick, and in the 1920s, it was the home of Tom Mix, a cowboy film star. "The estate... covers five landscaped acres. It includes a main house of 25 rooms, a guest house, swimming pool and pavilion, and a tennis court."[5]

As with the Bel-Air home, the young architect would reshape it to his modernist sensibility. Adam's mother would fill this, and subsequent homes, with beautiful, compelling art objects. These included, at various points in time, work by Matsumi (Mike) Kanemitsu, Georges Herms, Ynez Johnston, John Altoon, Joseph Cornell, Peter Voulkos, and Marcel Duchamp. Adam could pick up a Joseph Cornell box, designed to suggest a children's game, and give it a shake. Colorful, energetic Ynez Johnston paintings were part of his visual vocabulary, reflected in the ease in which he would fill a picture plane with symbolic shape and color. There are definite echoes of influence; a number of his drawings, especially of people and hands, hint at the loose line work of Herms and the psychological undertones of Altoon. An early abstract drawing from 1959 may have been inspired by Herms's assemblages or from Adam's young imagination (Figure 1.1).

Art was a daily activity, from a very early age. Adam's mother fondly recalled that the nursery schools—at least the private ones that her and her friends' children attended—had easels, tempera paints, and supplies for making sculptures and were well equipped for any budding young artist.[6] In addition, artists, particularly female artists, would offer art lessons. As a young boy, Adam studied art with Dorothy Royer and Catharine (Cathy) Anliss Heerman. Heerman and Julie had been classmates at Bennington College. Julie would bring home reams of typing paper for the children to cover with drawings, which she displayed along a long hallway in their home. Art became an obsession that Adam would have for his entire life. This is apparent in the extraordinary number of complex and fascinating drawings, prints, and films that he made throughout his life.

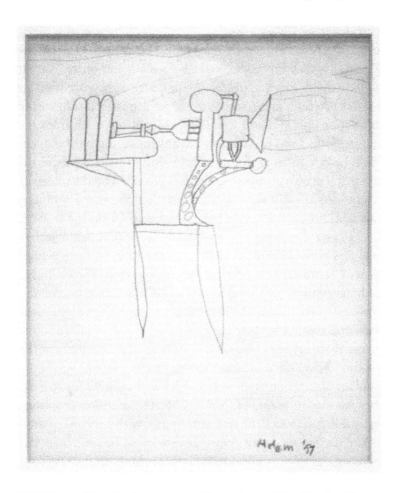

FIGURE 1.1   Drawing by a young Adam, dated 1959. (Used with permission from Beckett's family.)

His interest in animated images motivated his mother to have Jules Engel show films at Adam's eighth or ninth birthday party. She knew Engel through the art community; his abstract paintings were exhibited at established venues such as the Pasadena Museum of Art, the Paul Kantor Gallery in Beverly Hills, and the Whitney Museum of American Art in New York. He had contributed to Disney's *Fantasia*, and at the time of the party, he had been working with the innovative United Productions of America cartoon studio, right before moving on to Format Films in 1959. Engel appeared at the party, supplying films as well as a projector and screen. Julia remembers specifically seeing *Mr. McGoo* episodes and *Gerald McBoing-Boing*, both from the United Productions of America. Leaping forward 12 years, Adam would be in a room with Engel at the California Institute of the Arts with his own animated endeavors projected on the screen.

Julie also knew of the abstract animation of Oskar Fischinger, who, with his wife, Elfriede, had migrated to California in 1936, fleeing Nazi Germany. He had made numerous nonobjective films and was, by most accounts, the inspirational force behind Disney's *Fantasia*. Based on her recommendation, a screening of Fischinger's films was programmed as a fundraiser for Adam's school.[7] Unlike *Gerald McBoing-Boing*, these animations used shape and motion as their subject, showing synchronized forms diving, twirling, marching, and quivering. This was perhaps the first time Adam saw Fischinger's work.

Adam was an innately visual child and only began to read when he was 10 years old, perhaps because of vision problems. Once he began to read, he read voraciously, with a special passion for science fiction. As his drawings developed, he combined text and image, playing with words and their meanings, creating contrary juxtapositions, and flip-flopping phrases. This fascination with meaning and sound is evident in the titles of his films, such as *Heavy-Light, Knotte Grosse,* and *Kitsch in Synch*.

His earliest years as a student were at Westland School, a progressive school created in 1949 by parents and visionary educators. A core principle was that each child learned differently and at his or her own pace, which may have helped—or hindered—Adam with his reading difficulties. According to close childhood friends, his sister, and his mother, he had a healthy curiosity, was smart, and had numerous interests and talents, including music. He played the guitar from a fairly young age. He had a proclivity toward science and was adept at numerical computations. In fact, he made outstanding scores on his college entry tests and considered opting for math instead of art.[8]

Cathy Heerman's children, John and Victoria (Vicky), were about 3 months apart in age from Adam and Morgan, respectively. They were close friends from their earliest days. John remembers Adam at the Koenig house in Brentwood, when they were maybe only 1 or 2 years old; there were many visits between houses.[9] John's father was a record producer, and a love for music was a tie that the lifelong friends shared. John became a professional cellist, performing as a solo cellist in the Jerusalem symphony for a period and then as a member of the Swedish Radio Symphony in Stockholm. The house on Summit Drive is the first Beckett home that John remembers: it was opulent, with a rolling green lawn and a spectacular swimming pool. Even though it was immense and grand, it had an aura of disarray owing to the ongoing remodeling project. Adam liked to hike, and this was a common activity that he and John embarked on and an activity that was constant in Adam's life. His 1972 animation, *Dear Janice,* includes footage of a hike through the hills near his tiny house in Val Verde—a home quite different from the Summit Drive estate.

Adam's poor vision made activities such as catching a ball and navigating while running among a throng of playmates difficult, if not dangerous. He was larger than average and wore sizeable thick glasses, which gave him a studious air (Figure 1.2). Another childhood friend, Tom Schiller, remembers being at a summer camp with Adam, when they were around 9–12 years old. He recalls the kids from the camp hiking up Mount Whitney and that Adam "cut an interesting figure," looking more like an English schoolboy than an American one. "He was always an intriguing personality to me because he kept very solitary."[10] Toward the end of the day, they would often notice that Adam had left the group and was still up in the mountains, absorbed in trying to collect crystals from the rock. Immersed in his task, he would forget time, and someone

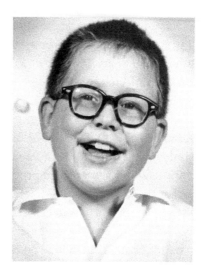

FIGURE 1.2 Adam as a young boy. (Used with permission from Beckett's family.)

would have to go to retrieve him. Schiller became one of the original writers for *Saturday Night Live* and wrote and produced a feature film, *Nothing Lasts Forever* (1984). The main character's name was Adam Beckett. He conveyed that the name had always struck him as being a great name, and he had respected Adam for being an odd character, navigating a world that was all his own.

Adam's early life offered every physical comfort and privilege, but there were problems. Some parents at Westland School objected to his "disruptive" behavior. His mother paid to have a special teacher brought in for 6 months, after which his rough patch of misbehavior seemed to have passed.[11] His mother recalls that he felt things intensely, not an uncommon trait for artists. John doesn't remember being intimidated by Adam, but his sister, Vicky's earliest memories of him were that he was large and had a temper. "He was kind of a bully, I think more from just kind of a passionate nature, but he really didn't know his own strength or the impact that he had physically. So he was a little intimidating to me as a little girl."[12]

Morgan, just months younger than Adam, was described as "stout-hearted." She would stand up to her older brother, and in their teens they would be described as co-conspirators. Deirdre, also spirited, was younger than Morgan by not quite a year. Younger and smaller, she often had to resort to yelling to make herself heard in the energetic Beckett household.

The root of Adam's anger and Deirdre's yelling may not be hard to trace. There were problems at home that undoubtedly impacted them. His parents were granted a divorce in June 1957. Adam was 7 years old. The grounds for the divorce, according to a brief article in the *Los Angeles Times* (June 13, 1957), were "extreme cruelty"[13] related to Mr. Beckett's "ungovernable temper" when under the influence of liquor. The children remained with their mother. Deirdre recalls that they would spend weekends with their father, and he would take them to the sites where his architectural designs were being built.

In July 1958, Julie Beckett married Digby Gallas, a medical doctor 20 years her senior. While his presence was a stabilizing influence, the family was uprooted from Beverly Hills, relocating to a home near the Inglewood area of Los Angeles, perhaps to be closer to Gallas's office located in a brand-new building on West Century Boulevard. The architect of that office was William S. Beckett.[14]

While William Beckett seemed somewhat eccentric and odd to Adam's young friends, Gallas was more involved with his family, and his high energy was a good match for Adam's exuberance. John remembers that Gallas would tickle the young Adam mercilessly and stop only when he would gasp "Sufficient!" Adam seemed to thrive with Gallas as his stepfather. He lost his chubbiness, and the thick-framed glasses were replaced with wire-rimmed ones.

The family moved to a new house on Sherbourne Drive in Inglewood, designed by the architect Gregory Ain and with a commissioned sculpture, "Gallas Rock," by Peter Voulkos, in the garden. Marina Gallas was born in January 1961, and Evan arrived the following year in July. Adam is described as being more focused and less intimidating during this time, undoubtedly due to Digby's influence and a more settled family life.

Westland School only went to sixth grade, so the Beckett children switched to public school, which must have seemed worlds away from their independent beginnings. He was in public school for a year and then enrolled in Oakwood School, returning to a progressive educational environment. This required a commute, as their secondary school campus was, at that time, located in Agoura, on the site of a summer camp.[15] The campus had opened in 1964, starting with grades seven through nine and then adding the upper grades as the classes progressed. He was one of only 40 or so students there.

Oakwood School, like Westland, was founded by parents and education reformers who were responding to overcrowded classrooms and authoritarian teaching styles. At Oakwood, learning was approached holistically, respecting individual learning styles and the overall development of the student. Deirdre recalls that the curriculum was challenging and motivating, with an emphasis on literature, especially poetry. Students were required to be active, critical learners and not to parrot the ideas of the teachers. Adam excelled and was nominated as an Oakwood student for a National Merit Scholarship in 1967.

It was there that he became friends with Mark Whitney, the son of pioneering filmmaker John Whitney, Sr. Mark was a free spirit in his own way. His mother, Jackie Whitney, a painter, had taken him out of public school after the vice principal had singled him out because of his long hair. His parents enrolled him in Oakwood, where individuality was encouraged. Along with Adam, Mark was one of nine students in the ninth-grade level. They connected immediately and developed a friendship that lasted throughout Adam's life. Mark recognized in Adam the antithesis of what he had experienced in his former high school. "I was fascinated by his authenticity and his idiosyncrasies.... He just had this level of being, this awkwardness—this deep awkwardness—that was cruel. And some people teased him... but... he was *fantastic*."[16]

Mark introduced Adam to the unique work of his father and his uncle, the artist James Whitney. The Whitney brothers made several films, both as a team and individually. This was a critical connection. Adam was able to witness the innovative and inventive approach to experimental film and motion graphics from his visits to the studio. John Whitney, Sr., engineered the equipment needed to manifest their visual theories and ideas. At the time Adam would have been at the Whitney's home, they had already completed a number of compelling abstract films, notably John's *Catalog*. The work he was doing would contribute heavily to the future motion graphics and visual effects industry. Mark Whitney confirms that his father's films intrigued Adam. "He always had notebooks and did a lot of drawing. And at a certain point that jumped into the idea of animating them. I actually think that his connection to seeing the films and having some conversations with my father may have been instrumental in that part of his creative process." Six years later, in an interview by Robert Russett for the seminal text *Experimental Animation*, Adam credited John Whitney, Sr., as one of several artists who influenced him.[17] Several mandala-like stencils found in Adam's materials, with images made by using them, were probably inspired by the disks that Whitney used on his motion control device, built from repurposed military surplus equipment (Figure 1.3).

While Adam was growing up immersed in the physical comforts of wealth, surrounded by intellectual adults, and attending progressive schools, this was not the experience for many in the United States. Change was happening. The 1961 failed Bay of Pigs invasion revealed questionable government activities. A group of Cuban exiles, armed and trained by the Central Intelligence Agency (CIA), tried to oust the new Cuban dictator, Fidel Castro, and failed publicly. In 1963, President Kennedy was assassinated, and the news of the shooting was broadcast immediately via television to a shocked nation, which watched, transfixed, as the

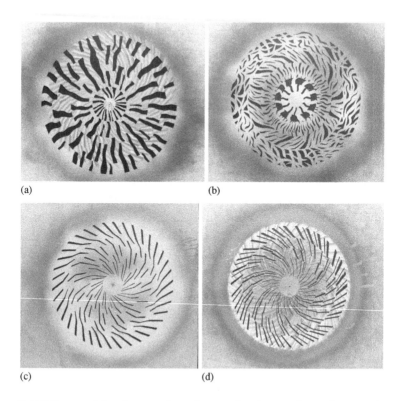

(a)　　　　　　　　　　(b)

(c)　　　　　　　　　　(d)

FIGURE 1.3 Adam's stencils, echoing the discs John Whitney, Sr. used with his motion control machine. (a) Stencil with paint showing layering of color and pattern. (b) Stencil with bands of curved lines. (c) Stencil with yellow paint. (d) Stencil showing layers of paint and pattern in opposing directions. (Used with permission from Beckett's family.)

news unfolded over the next few days. Two days after the assassinations, those watching NBC's ongoing television coverage saw Lee Harvey Oswald shot dead by Jack Ruby, while surrounded by policemen.

Civil unrest grew, as inequalities became glaringly obvious and unacceptable. African American families were kept out of neighborhoods by unfair real estate practices and racist threats. There was an urgent cry for access to equal education, resulting in the

Civil Rights Act of 1964, which outlawed segregation of all forms. In Los Angeles, tensions erupted in August 1965, as the black community of Watts responded to police aggression, resulting in what is now remembered as the Watts riots.

Like many residents of America, Dr. Gallas was disturbed by the Bay of Pigs invasion in 1961 and concerned about the country's civil unrest. Named Isidoros Xinogalas at birth, he grew up in Alexandria, Egypt. His name was changed to Digby Gallas when the family immigrated to America.[18] Grateful for his own opportunities, Gallas wanted to make a positive contribution to society. He volunteered to work as a physician for the Peace Corps. His assignment was in India, where he would assist rural women with family planning, making an alternative form of birth control available to them and educating them in its use. Unlike some of the other doctors, Gallas took his wife and children with him on his mission. Adam's youngest siblings Marina and Evan were just 4 and 3 years old, respectively. They departed from Los Angeles in the summer of 1965, stopping in North Carolina for orientation and inoculations.[19] Adam was 15 years old and up for an adventure. Reportedly, only his sister Morgan protested, as she was 14 years old and was leaving friends at a crucial time in her adolescence.

Mysticism and Eastern spirituality had been introduced to Western culture in the 1950s, particularly on the West Coast, through the writings of the beatniks, such as Gary Snyder and Kenneth Rexroth, and the radio broadcast talks of the pop philosopher and author Alan Watts, which started in 1953. There was a fairly diverse population in California at that time, and the liberal schooling of the three older children would have provided a good foundation. But India—especially rural India—in the mid-1960s would definitely have been an adventure for this liberal, well-to-do family from Los Angeles. To those who knew the family, it seemed that they had disappeared—they were gone so long.

They arrived in New Delhi and then set out to a remote rural village. There wasn't a choice of schools. Adam attended a Jesuit school, and his sisters went to a convent school. Not only was there an educational authority at the front of the classroom but also a religious one! Deirdre, who was now 13 years old, remembers eating lunch out in the schoolyard, watched by the nuns, while large buzzards circled overhead. One day, a buzzard swooped down and grabbed Deirdre's sandwich. She was doubly startled when a nun ran out with a shotgun and shot into the air to scare away the scavengers.[20]

The family visited nearby villages occasionally and even went north to Katmandu, Nepal, for a long weekend. They found it full of refugees, some selling banners, which they kept rolled up and hidden under their garments. Julie bought a banner that was a depiction of the Tibetan pantheon.[21] This foray into the culture around them exposed the children to Eastern philosophy, as it was experienced and practiced on a daily basis, as well as to completely different ways of living and being. It also expanded Adam's visual vocabulary.

Rather than returning home directly, they toured parts of the Mediterranean and Europe, taking nearly 3 months to do so. Gallas was interested in his heritage, so they did a complete tour of Greece, visiting some of the more remote areas. They also went to Egypt, boating out onto the Nile River in a traditional felucca, which provided a wonderful vantage point for viewing the temples and other ancient structures.

In Europe, Paris was their main destination, and they enthusiastically explored its numerous art galleries, museums, and antiquities. The teenaged Adam was tall and slim, no longer the large, bespectacled schoolboy, and he still preferred to explore by himself, which was undoubtedly easier than negotiating with his parents and four siblings. Adam's tendency to prefer solitude is a trait that he carried into his later years.

Treasures—Indian prints, fabrics, and figurines—were collected along the way to take home, adding to the art that filled their house and colored their daily experience. The varied figures and the active, filled surfaces would influence Adam's

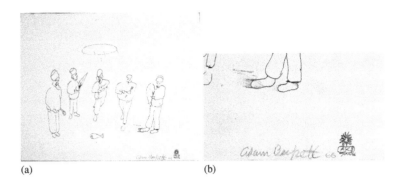

(a)   (b)

FIGURE 1.4 (a) Sketch of a scene during his travels, dated 1966. (b) Signature and mark for "AKB." (Used with permission from Beckett's family.)

drawings and the complex, abstracted space of his animations. His experience of the world was now larger and enriched from witnessing different cultures with their mysteries and relics, exploring ancient cities, and visiting prominent museums. He became considerably more mature and focused as an artist during his travels.[22] His sketches from that time exhibit a variety of styles, often in watercolor, of quickly captured impressions filtered through his imagination (Figure 1.4).

BIBLIOGRAPHY

House and Home. "Regency Remodeled: A Modern Architect Treats the Past and the Present with Respect," *House and Home,* May 1952, V.1.

Kansas City Times. "Wife to Pay Alimony," *Kansas City Times,* June 13, 1957. https://www.newspapers.com/image/50991827.

Los Angeles Times. "Former Tom Mix Estate Purchased by Architect," *Los Angeles Times,* March 17, 1954. ProQuest Historical Newspapers, *Los Angeles Times* (1881–1985).

Los Angeles Times. "Wife, Divorced, Agrees to Pay Architect Mate," *Los Angeles Times,* June 13, 1957, 4. ProQuest Historical Newspapers, *Los Angeles Times* (1881–1985).

Marsh, Jessie Jean. "William Beckett Extend Invitation to Fete Saturday," Society, *Los Angeles Times,* December 30, 1953. ProQuest Historical Newspapers, *Los Angeles Times* (1881–1985).

Peace Corps Volunteer newsletter, October 1965. http://peacecorpson-line.org/historyofthepeacecorps/primarysources/19651001%20 Volunteer_Oct.pdf.

Russett, Robert and Cecile Starr. 1976. *Experimental Animation: An Illustrated Anthology.* New York: Van Nostrand Reinhold.

Youngblood, Gene. 1970. *Expanded Cinema.* New York: Dutton & Co. http://www.vasulka.org/Kitchen/PDF_ExpandedCinema/book.pdf.

ENDNOTES

[1] John Hanhardt, in discussion with the author (phone), July 19, 2005.

[2] Deirdre Beckett, interview by the author, August 17, 2004.

[3] Marsh, Jessie Jean. "William Beckett Extend Invitation to Fete Saturday," Society, *Los Angeles Times*, December 30, 1953, B3.

[4] "Regency Remodeled: A Modern Architect Treats the Past and the Present with Respect," *House and Home*, May 1952, V.1. 152–155.

[5] "Former Tom Mix Estate Purchased by Architect," *Los Angeles Times*, March 17, 1954, 23.

[6] Julianne (Julie) Kemper Beckett (Gilliam), interview by the author, July 26, 2006. Gilliam was her last name at time of interview.

[7] Ibid.

[8] D. Beckett, Ibid.

[9] John Koenig, in discussion with the author (phone), June 21, 2006.

[10] Tom Schiller, in discussion with the author (phone), September 24, 2005.

[11] Julie Gilliam, Ibid.

[12] Victoria (Vicky) Koenig, in discussion with the author (phone), August 24, 2005.

[13] "Wife to Pay Alimony," *Kansas City Times*, June 13, 1957, 1. https://www.newspapers.com/image/50994827, and "Wife, Divorced, Agrees to Pay Architect Mate," *Los Angeles Times*, June 13, 1957, 4.

[14] Article 7—No Title, *Los Angeles Times*, January 20, 1957, F10. Photograph with caption regarding the "New Lennox Facility" a new facility for Westchester Medical Group, which included Dr. Digby Gallas, and citing the architect of the over $100,000 project as William S. Beckett.

[15] Oakwood website, http://www.oakwoodschool.org/. Retrieved January 8, 2005.

[16] Mark Whitney, interview by the author, April 12, 2003.

[17] Robert Russett, "Adam Beckett" in *Experimental Animation*, Robert Russett and Cecile Starr (New York: Van Nostrand Reinhold, 1976), 11. Interview of Beckett was on November 1974.

[18] Evan Gallas, email to the author, January 30, 2007.

[19] *Peace Corps Volunteer* newsletter, October 1965, 29. http://peacecorpsonline.org/historyofthepeacecorps/primarysources/19 651001%20Volunteer_Oct.pdf. It notes that Dr. Gallas and sixteen other doctors were participants in the summer training program at Duke University and includes a photograph of Marina getting a vaccination.

[20] D. Beckett, Ibid.

[21] Julie Gilliam, Ibid.

[22] John Koenig, email to author, August 28, 2018.

CHAPTER 2

Transitions

Adam in Motion

A DAM'S FAMILY RETURNED TO a changed world. America had crossed the threshold from civil discontent into a cultural revolution. The first wave of baby boomers, born after the end of World War II, were now young adults and entering a society that did not align with the contrived reality seen in the advertisements with which they had grown up in the 1950s. They were living with political and social stress created by the optimism of postwar economic growth set against the dark cloud of the Cold War.

The family had no time to readjust to this strange homecoming before tragedy struck. On October 10, 1966, soon after their return home, Dr. Gallas suddenly died of a heart attack. He was only 59 years old. It was a crushing blow to the family; their foundation was gone, and Julie was now a single mom with five children. Adam was 16 years old and had just lost the stability that his stepfather of 9 years had provided. Undoubtedly, Dr. Gallas would have been a lifeline in the coming weeks and years when drugs and various personalities interjected themselves into Adam's young life. His loss magnified the disruption that their travels had caused for the Beckett siblings, as adolescents who were developing a sense of self within their peer community.

Adam's generation came of age in a culture that was significantly different from that of their parents, creating a distance, or a "generation gap," in perceptions of social and political realities. The need for change held urgency for these young adults, and they actively rebelled against the authorities who wielded power but could no longer be respected or trusted. The government could no longer credibly portray itself as the protective moral entity as it now appeared determined to become the "Big Brother" that George Orwell had forewarned of in his novel *Nineteen Eighty-Four*. Rejecting the status quo, the new generation sought to create an alternative, and a counterculture was born in the United States. Similar changes and conflicts were happening around the world.

Dorgie Bonds was one of the earliest members of the communal entourage called the Hog Farm family, a group that would soon play an important role in Adam's life. She describes the disenchantment that she and many of her peers experienced at the time.

> ... they told us everything was perfect and wonderful. And we actually believed that people that were hungry were fed by people that had enough, you know what I mean?! We really believed the golden rule and America saved the universe.... So when we got to be thinking adults and found out we had been so horribly lied to... we just freaked out. And we threw everything out the window. Everything.[1]

The radio was playing "California Dreamin" and "Monday, Monday" by the Mamas and the Papas, Nancy Sinatra's "These Boots Are Made for Walking," and The Rolling Stones' "Paint It Black." The Beatles *Revolver* album was released with the hits "Yellow Submarine," "Paperback Writer," and "Eleanor Rigby." Freedom of expression in clothing abandoned the color and forms of the 1950s. Young "hippies" sported headbands, necklaces, fringed vests, bell-bottom jeans, and brightly colored fabrics with paisley and iconic pop graphics. Skirts were mini, maxi, and midi in length, in everything from mod to free-flowing shapes. Young men grew their hair long, in opposition to the buzzed cuts of the military or "straights." And, perhaps, most disturbing to parents of teenagers, drugs became an accepted part of the emerging counterculture.

Marijuana had been around for decades and became popular again in the 1960s; however, it was illegal to possess. Lysergic acid diethylamide (LSD) was a newer and different kind of drug. It was legal in California until late 1966, around the time when Adam's family returned to the States. Unlike marijuana, or "pot," LSD was synthesized and induced psychedelic experiences. Actor Cary Grant spoke publicly of the positive and life-changing impact that the drug had on him. A 1966 art exhibit titled "LSD Art" at Riverside Museum in New York City was featured as the September cover story for *Life* magazine.[2] The accompanying photographs documented art that was transcendental and psychedelic, with colored lights, lenses, and other means to alter the senses while experiencing the work. Timothy Leary, a psychologist who had worked with LSD experimentation, became a proponent of its use, and in 1966, he invited a generation to "tune in, turn on, and drop out." The young generation heeded the call, and the government that had once experimented actively with the drug for possible military uses scrambled to respond. By 1968, it was illegal in all 50 states.

Free love was also a popular mantra of the time. A "sexual revolution" was in full swing, as young people redefined relationships, often rejecting monogamy as a constraint. Women could exercise more control of their bodies with the legalization of birth control pills for contraceptive use in 1960 in some states. Bonds, in recalling what that generation "threw out the window," noted that monogamy was one thing that was often discarded, which perhaps should not have been, because it was something that actually made life run a little smoother.[3]

Along with equal rights and civil rights, America's escalating participation in the war in Vietnam impacted and alarmed Adam's generation. By 1968, as he was graduating from Oakwood, 536,100 were fighting the Viet Cong and North Vietnamese.[4] Protests against America's involvement in the war were accelerated by an increase in deployed troops and fueled by television coverage; it was the first war to be broadcast on television.

Adam's family had returned near the start of school, and that was a distraction for the children, as they reintegrated with some of their peers and returned to a routine. Julie was left to reassemble their lives and somehow navigate the new cultural landscape. The impact of that time seemed etched upon her memory, as she recounted listening to the radio late one night. Not being able to sleep, she decided to unpack some of their footlockers that had arrived from India. She tuned in to a talk show on the public radio station, KPFK, and was astounded to hear young people calling in and discussing LSD, or acid, asking the best way to find this drug and advice on what to do while dropping acid. She remembers:

> I couldn't unpack the footlocker anymore. I just sat down on one of the dining room chairs and listened.... I thought, well, I've got to come right out and meet this. I can't stay at home and say it's not happening, children don't go there, don't do this! I've got to accept it and have people over and find out as much as I can about it.[5]

Endeavoring to learn and embrace the change, she went to see avant-garde films, such as the work of Kenneth Anger. She opened up her home to an assortment of people and encouraged her children to bring their friends home. She laughed, remembering, "I had some pretty strange people in my living room." Her living room was now in a different house. Sometime in 1967, they moved to La Mesa Drive in Santa Monica.

The home that was filled with art and that would normally host people in the Los Angeles art scene was now filled with young artists and people who were rejecting society and trying to live life on their own terms—a spirit not alien to Julie or the Beckett teenagers. They often had people staying with them as they were passing through or that needed temporary shelter. Gene Flores, the sculptor whose work stands as a memorial to Adam in Barnsdall Park, noted that she collected art and "took in wandering, stray artists."[6] He and his wife stayed there when they were in town. Friends remember seeing people in the house sort of hovering around, just slightly offstage. It was usually unclear what their connection was to the family, but they seemed to belong. Adam's mother admits that he "didn't see the usual kind of people when he was growing up. He knew some pretty exotic people."

In this flow of people, Julie met two young women who would greatly influence the direction of their lives, Russell Ann (Rusty) Gilliam and Jean (Oxygen) Nichols. Rusty was the older sister of Michelle Phillips of the Mamas and the Papas. Oxygen and her husband at that time, Peter Whiterabbit, lived with Rusty and worked for the band when needed. Both young women helped Julie, looking after Evan and Marina, who were now 5 and 6 years old, and sometimes driving the older kids around. Julie met Rusty's father, Gardner Burnett Gilliam, and he and Julie became close friends, accompanying each other to museums and movies. He had been a merchant marine captain and had a large personality to balance her own. Later, in 1975, they got married.

At Oakwood School, the Beckett siblings were regarded as distinctive, even in this place full of unique teenagers. Their disappearance to India had enhanced this perception of them. Carl Stone, who would later provide a sound score for one of Adam's animations, was one of Deirdre's classmates. He recalls Adam from Oakwood: "Even in a school of sort of hippie oddballs, he was the oddest of the hippiest of them. He always had his guitar, I remember. He always had great clothes and he just seemed like a nice sort of free spirit and a friendly guy."[7] The family had joined the counterculture almost without effort.

As the summer of 1967 loomed ahead, Julie decided to get the children out of Los Angeles, joining the many who were traveling at that time. Young people were flooding San Francisco's Haight-Ashbury neighborhood, even as Scott McKenzie sang "San Francisco (Be Sure to Wear Flowers in Your Hair)," which was released in May 1967. There was hope for change, and something exciting was in the air. As Oxygen notes, "... we felt like we were changing the world, or we were rejecting a lot of what was going on in society."[8] That summer became "The Summer of Love."

Julie bought an old school bus and, with her daughters, Oxygen, and another friend, transformed it into a mobile home, as numerous others were doing. They outfitted the bus, and when the children were out of school that summer, they headed north, with a mission to find a totem pole carver (Figure 2.1). The family had never been further north than San Francisco. Their quest led them to Jimmy Kaluga, a carver from the Kwakiutl tribe, in Canada, and she commissioned him to make her a totem pole.

The events from that summer are somewhat of a blur. Based on stories woven together from pieces told by Deirdre Beckett, Julie, Oxygen, and Peri Fleischmann (Peter Whiterabbit's mother),

FIGURE 2.1 Sketch from 1967, perhaps created while traveling on the bus. (Used with permission from Beckett's family.)

it is clear that the whole family came along on the journey, and Fleischmann recalls being on the bus at some point too. It probably took the group to the now-famous Monterey Pop Festival, credited by many with being the world's first major rock concert. "Papa" John Phillips was a key organizer of the festival. Z'ev, a musician and a friend of the Beckett siblings, recalls that, later in college, Adam wasn't into LSD but professed to have had his ultimate acid trip at Big Sur in the summer of 1967, when he was 17 years old (Figure 2.2).[9] Big Sur is just south of the Monterey Fairgrounds, where the musicians converged that summer.

The bus that Julie purchased ultimately wound up belonging to Whiterabbit and Oxygen. They used the bus to bring Jimmy Kaluga (Chief Jimmy King) and the totem pole back to Los Angeles.[10] At the end of 1967, Jimmy Kaluga and the much-awaited totem pole arrived at their home on La Mesa Drive. The raising of the totem pole in the family's front yard was a grand event—a "mad celebration" according to Julie—with musicians playing and Jimmy Kaluga in Native regalia. Oxygen recounts the event:

> Jimmy King in his chief robe—a beautiful red and black cape with shells on it—with his "talking stick." I remember that he got a little drunk and went off about the treatment of Native Americans here. He had always thought US Indians were treated better than Canadians and then discovered otherwise. My memory—perhaps partly fantasy—was that he forcefully planted his chief talking stick making a point and a few miles away at the coast, a piece of the Santa Monica hills slid into the ocean. Maybe a common mudslide but I attributed it to his vehemence. Peter had a tooth worked on—maybe extracted—by a dentist at the party. It was quite an event... as were many during those years.[11]

Eric Saarinen documented the event on film and recalls Michelle Phillips being there along with a diverse assortment of young

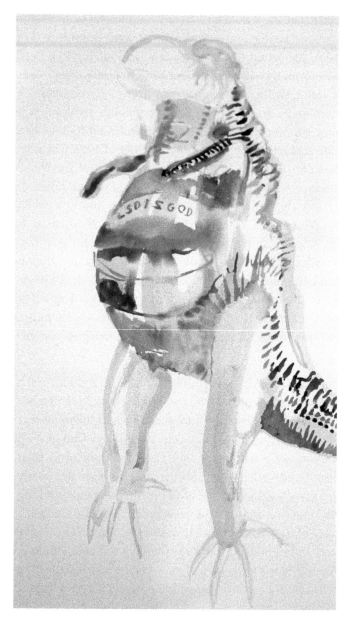

FIGURE 2.2 Adam's editorial drawing on LSD, circa 1967. (Used with permission from Beckett's family.)

people.[12] A watercolor by Adam, executed in a brilliant brown, yellow, and orange palette, is also likely a record of the event, signed and dated 1967. It's a loosely executed painting depicting three people in a semicircle, with the central figure representing the totem pole artist, Jimmy Kaluga. He is wearing a large feathered headdress (although the Kwakiutl don't wear feather headdresses) and has a staff in one hand. A nude female has an orange body, as if illuminated by fire. She has large, awkward feet, and her arms stretch out on both sides. Her mouth is open, perhaps because she is singing. The third person, while mostly nude, wears some sort of wrap with spots, possibly indicating fur, and they hold what is probably a pipe (Figure 2.3).

Adam returned to Oakwood for his senior year and continued to excel in his studies there. In an age where dropping out and turning on were the mantra, he stayed in school. His friend Mark Whitney, his sister Morgan, and many others did "drop out,"

FIGURE 2.3 Watercolor inspired by the totem pole ceremony, 1967. (Used with permission from Beckett's family.)

electing to get a high school equivalency certificate. In the fall of 1967, Adam was nominated as a semi-finalist for a national merit scholarship. In the spring of 1968, Oakwood School graduated its first class of students, which included Adam. He was recruited to create the cover for the graduation program. Perhaps, the gravity of the transitional ceremony inspired his design, along with tales of a natural childbirth told by Rusty. It was a four-panel comic page, showing students on stage in front of a proud audience. The second, and rather large, panel depicts newly formed adults, including a female wearing a skirt but with uncovered breasts, emerging from a large womb-like creature, the mother womb of Oakwood (Figure 2.4). His design wasn't used.

Adam applied to numerous colleges; his admission test scores were high, and he had many options of where to attend. Deirdre remembers that their father took Adam to interviews at the

FIGURE 2.4 Oakwood School 1968 graduation program designed by Adam (not used). (Used with permission from Beckett's family.)

prospective colleges. He chose Antioch College in Yellow Springs, Ohio, and entered as an art student in the summer quarter of 1968. In the late 1960s, Antioch was known as one of the several leading liberal colleges and was a Midwestern cultural hotbed for young radicals. His records indicate that he was there in late July for the summer quarter, receiving his first course evaluations in September.

Adam probably traveled with the group known as the Hog Farm in the first months of the summer of 1968. Oxygen and Whiterabbit were connected to the group, and through them, the bus became the family's link to the communal group. Commandeered by Whiterabbit, the "Queen's Midtown Tunnel of Love," as the bus was named, joined the many other buses that toured around the country to events in an ever-evolving caravan. David Lebrun, filmmaker and member, worked on light shows and described the group, and the experience, as a "multimedia circus."[13] The abstraction and innovation of the light shows had to have made an impact on Adam.

The Hog Farm originated from an actual hog farm in Tujunga, California, north of Burbank in the hills, and while there was no authoritarian leadership, the revered ringmaster was, and still is, Hugh Romney, better known as Wavy Gravy. In his book *The Hog Farm and Friends*, he describes the group as "an expanded family, a mobile hallucination, a sociological experiment, an army of clowns. We are 50 people on a perpetual trip, with six converted school buses, some vans and pickups, one for our pet pig, Pigasus, who now weighs 400 pounds and has learned to roll over."[14] This "army of clowns" would converge at concerts or rallies and assist with publicity, light shows, crowd management, and cleanup. Each of them filled niches, as needed and able; some cooked, some were mechanics, and some created and ran the light shows.

The summer of 1968 was a busy one for the Hog Farm family. A new commune for the group was being negotiated in New Mexico and at some point, Oxygen, now sometimes called Djinn, and Whiterabbit joined the group there. Dorgie Bonds described a "pied piper" effect, as the caravan of buses grew, and more people crowded onto the buses.[15] Increasingly, disaffected young people looked for an alternative life and kindred spirits and were attracted to the group, as it gained notoriety.

People changed buses, and buses separated and reconnected during the journeys that took them to New York, Detroit, and the infamous Democratic National Convention in Chicago. The convention was held from August 26 through 29, and Adam was there. Deirdre remembers that he was one of the many people arrested, maybe because he was carrying a box of art supplies of some sort and "appeared suspicious." Purportedly, too, this is where he got his beloved canine companion, Elvis. Adam includes a report of his arrest in his Antioch College course review to his "preceptor," Jim Jordan. Antioch had abolished grades in July of 1968 and opted for course reports from students and faculty. Adam's humor and irreverence are apparent as he describes his ordeal.

> I had my biggest run-in with the machinery this quarter, too. I went to Chicago for the Convention. It was really nice, not too warm, a nice breeze, plenty of congenial people... It was rather unpleasant too; a little tear gas is really uh-mace-ing, as they say, and too many police spoil the bone structure. I got arrested for no crime, beat up with a complete Gestapo vocabulary of horror tricks and words and released without glasses, spryness or usual good humor, all to be quickly regained excepting the glasses, but dots annuduh story.[16]

A unique aspect of the Antioch College curriculum was that it required students to spend whole school terms out of class and in a cooperative study, or a co-op, situation. Co-ops were done off-campus with nonprofit organizations, artists, studios or whatever offered a good match for the student's path of study. His records indicate that his co-op work was with the Art Students League, in New York, during the spring and summer of 1969. There are no review notes about his experience. Perhaps, Adam used that time to travel or perhaps, he was at the Art Students League only for a short while. No one recalls him being in New York during this time, except for his trip to Woodstock. However, one of his comics is titled "The Subway Ride" and shows a nude couple descending into the city's subway. The entrance is a large tongue emerging from an open mouth. The next panel shows a sign "NYC Subway Poor People's Entrance," and the mouth, now closed, says "Ummh!" The couple tumbles downward and ends up in "subway land," which seems quite empty (Figure 2.5).

A "Gathering of the Tribes" was held at Aspen Meadows, near Santa Fe, New Mexico, at the Summer Solstice (June 21)

FIGURE 2.5 Comic drawing, "The Subway Ride." (Used with permission from Beckett's family.)

in 1969. A flyer announcing that event was among Adam's artifacts and the drawing style and composition—and the signature of "Ambrose Fierce"—indicate that Adam was the artist or
designer and undoubtedly in attendance (Figure 2.6). A month
later, a photograph confirms his presence at the commune in
Llano, New Mexico, on Sunday, July 20, 1969. In it, we see a tall,
thin Adam with long hair, wearing a wide-brimmed hat, standing a bit awkwardly, with a thumb hooked in his jeans' pocket.
He is wearing work boots, with his jeans rolled mid-calf. There
is a softball game—of sorts—in progress. Oxygen recalls that
they had three televisions set up, as the first moon landing
occurred that same day; they were celebrating. A description
of this game appears in Wavy Gravy's book; the photograph is
attributed to Oxygen.[17]

The group was enlisted to help out with clearing the land and
for general organization and assistance during the now-mythical
Woodstock festival. The story goes that, on landing, they were
met by the media and informed that they were to provide secu-
rity. When asked what they were using as weapons, Wavy, with
his pacifist logic, responded, "Seltzer bottles and cream pie.[18] The
group was extremely busy at Woodstock, providing for the basic
needs of the thousands of people that converged on that infamous
weekend. They had the food tent, from which granola was distributed, and the "freak out tent" for people who were having bad
trips. While it's pretty certain that a young Adam was there with
the group, it's not known if he was on the bus or went by plane, and
strangely, he doesn't seem to have shared thoughts or details about
his experience there.

Oxygen only has dim memories of Adam. He was not the
imposing presence that he later became but was still the absorbed
loner that Mark Whitney remembers from Oakwood, not shy but
just doing his own thing. Lebrun confirmed Adam's association

FIGURE 2.6   Summer Solstice poster, 1969. (Used with permission from Beckett's family.)

with the group and Evan Gallas still maintains a connection to members. Knowing of Adam's experience with this group sheds light on some of his drawings, comics, and a few flyers that he designed. He rarely talked much about his time with the Hog Farm family, and many close friends were surprised to hear of his affiliation.

Traveling up the West Coast and cross-country, in the midst of the cultural revolution, would be an adventure for a young man. Adam's adventures on the bus began when he was 17 years old. Even though he was energetic and adventurous, it is likely that he was off in his own world and somewhat reclusive, as when he was a youngster at the summer camp, on a solo mission, seeking out crystals. Everything was an experiment as he ventured out, barely an adult, and everyone around him was navigating new territory. Drugs were readily available and were a large part of the experience. His friend Mark Whitney recalls, "Adam said on several occasions to me that he felt that he had been victimized by the pharmaceuticals that were so readily available at that period of time, and he didn't have the guidance or the mentoring to steer his way through that."[19]

His grounding force was his art. Vicky Koenig remembers that Adam drew obsessively. "He'd draw... he was always doing it. It was just a force of nature, kind of uncontainable. He couldn't fit into... his body. He was never settled inside of himself."[20] He created comic book pages, sketches, doodles, and posters. He referred to his background as graphic arts in an interview several years later, and Deirdre recalls that one of their favorite books was of the Fillmore's concert posters.[21]

A comic page entitled "Drawn on a Bus Comet" is dated 1969 and is signed as Algernon Picayune, his most-used pseudonym. Here, his black ink drawings are detailed, fantastic, and complex. Unlike "The Subway Ride," mentioned earlier, which is loosely drawn but has clearly decipherable text, space, and people, the characters in the "Bus Comet" piece are entities, not distinguishable as humans. The page is a mass of textured lines with slashes,

FIGURE 2.7 "Drawn on a Bus Comet," comic page. (Used with permission from Beckett's family.)

dots, and squiggles, defining the subjects who point up at the sky and speak in gibberish (Figure 2.7). The comic panels are drawn in fairly angular shapes, organically containing the images and filling the page. The last panel is particularly beautiful, with the two entities standing on a hill, their shadows dark behind them, and the sky filled with stars and a comet. The moon is cropped, so we only see the mouth and bottom of the nose; the mouth is closed and content.

It is likely that many of his sketchbooks came from this time period as he responded to what was around on the buses and at events. A few are obviously from drawing classes. Adam used diverse styles and media in these books; gouache or watercolor, ink, and pencil. There are straightforward figure drawings and more imaginative interpretations of figures, where limbs dissolve or merge with another figure or the landscape. In the numerous

nude figures, he demonstrates that he can draw well, by classi-
cal standards. Proportion, form, light, and line, all are composed
in images that are technically correct and aesthetically pleasing.
Looser, quick sketches in gouache show an eye for shape and
gesture, with just a few lines clearly communicating a motion, a
female form. And then, there are the fantastic interpretations that
have more of a narrative quality as people cavort, usually nude, or
whose features or bodies blend with those of animals (Figure 2.8).
These all speak to an avid imagination, fueled by the activity
around him and possibly by a drug-altered rendering of his imag-
ined and experienced worlds.

His reputation as an emerging artist led to a few known com-
missions for graphic art projects. Lester Koenig was a record producer, and, through his son John's insistence, he enlisted Adam
to create the album cover for Huey "Sonny" Simmons's 1970
recording "Burning Spirits." (John was credited as the associate
producer.) It was a colorful, abstract, meditative design of spheres
in circles and in squares that seemed to be receding into the center space. He had created the cover based on his experience of
Simmons's music.[22] A second project was the design of a poster

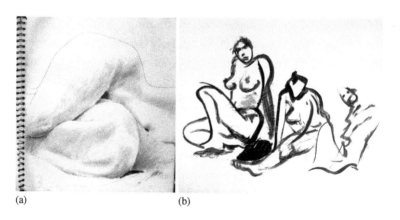

(a) (b)

FIGURE 2.8   (a) Life drawing that demonstrates Adam's ability to draw
the human form. (b) Quick sketches of the female form.   (*Continued*)

(c)

FIGURE 2.8 (Continued) (c) Imaginative composition that shows a human form morphing into the landscape and abstraction. (Used with permission from Beckett's family.)

for the Mamas and the Papas (Figure 2.9). His graphic skills were well known and his connection to Oxygen and Rusty put him in proximity to the Mamas and the Papas. The elements that he used to create the poster are among the artifacts that he left behind.

At the same time when he was considering himself a graphic artist in high school, he was being introduced to diverse moving-image

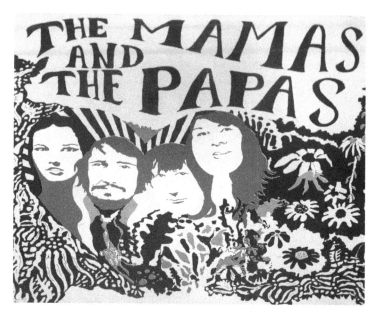

FIGURE 2.9 Detail from a screen print for a Mamas and Papas poster. (Used with permission from Beckett's family.)

media. There were the light shows created by artists with the Hog Farm, produced by light manipulation techniques such as oil wipe and also projections of experimental film. As noted by Oxygen, he probably saw the direct film work of the avant-garde filmmaker Harry Smith, who she and Whiterabbit knew well.[23] This added to his earlier firsthand knowledge of the abstract animations of the Whitneys. And, in a 1974 interview with Robert Russett, Adam mentioned that he did some cutout paper animation while in high school.[24] It was likely that he saw the stop-motion experiments of Cathy Heerman, perhaps learning from her the basics of how to animate.

Heerman was a pivotal figure in Adam's precollege years, and as he transitioned to adulthood. She was a successful artist and taught at the Junior Arts Center at Barnsdall Park. According to fellow instructor Libby Chaney, she would often host a simple dinner of spaghetti, chili, or perhaps a turkey on Wednesday nights, inviting other instructors.[25] Heerman was an enthusiastic supporter and advocate of Adam and his art, and he would sometimes be at these dinners. She also championed another artist, a young man named James Gore, who, like Adam, drew compulsively. James also wrote poetry. Vicky Koenig recalls, "They didn't draw... they breathed and it all poured out. It wasn't like they were making drawings, it was like part of their psyche."[26]

Gore and Adam became friends, perhaps after meeting at one of the Wednesday night get-togethers. Heerman was the link, as confirmed by Gore's former wife, Eve De Bona.[27] While Adam was a big guy and seemed uncomfortable in his body, Gore was attractive, slender, and graceful. He was also making animations.

Adam acknowledged seeing Gore's "fantastic films" before he headed off to Antioch College and said that those films inspired him to make a connection between his "graphic work" and filmmaking.[28] The films by Gore that Adam referred to are now lost, at least at the time of this writing, and it is intriguing to wonder what those may have been. Gore's known films are *Dream of the Sphinx*, *A Letter to a Friend* (now referred to as *The Letter*), and a lesser-known *6shortfilms* (1973).[29] *The Letter*, while heavily driven by Gore's raw drawing style and surreal imagery, was a collaboration with Adam and includes a section that demonstrates an early incarnation of the evolving cycle, for which Adam became known. *6shortfilms* includes some of Gore's drawings for *The Letter* but does not demonstrate the brilliant, surreal narrative seen in the other two animations. It is possible that *Dream of the Sphinx* was made earlier, before Adam left for Antioch, and then revamped to enter into the 1971 Annecy Festival in France.

The influences in moving-image art motivated Adam to include film in his studies at Antioch, and it was there that he turned his drawing obsession toward animation. It was experimental cinema that motivated him to animate, not cartoons. The first-year summary sheet from Antioch shows his coursework included ethics, calculus, printmaking, drawing, and an independent study in "film, readings, music." His "Stage III-Extramural" lists the employer as "self" and the job title as "animator."

BIBLIOGRAPHY

Cosgrove, Ben. "Trip the Light Fantastic with LSD-Inspired Art," *Life. Time*, October 7, 2014. http://time.com/3881126/lsd-inspired-art-photos/.

Gravy, Wavy. 1974. *The Hog Farm and Friends*. New York: Links Books.

Russett, Robert and Cecile Starr. 1976. *Experimental Animation: An Illustrated Anthology*. New York: Van Nostrand Reinhold.

Youngblood, Gene. 1970. *Expanded Cinema*. New York: Dutton & Co. http://www.vasulka.org/Kitchen/PDF_ExpandedCinema/book.pdf.

ENDNOTES

[1] Dorgie Bonds, discussion with the author, March 13, 2007.

[2] Ben Cosgrove. "Trip the Light Fantastic with LSD-Inspired Art, *Life. Time*, October 7, 2014. http://time.com/3881126/lsd-inspired-art-photos/.

[3] Bonds, Ibid.

[4] U.S. Department of Commerce, Bureau of the Census, "Vietnam Conflict—U.S. Military Forces in Vietnam and Casualties Incurred: 1965 to 1972," table 428, *Statistical Abstract of the United States, 1973* (Washington, DC: U.S. Department of Commerce, Social and Economic Statistics Administration, Bureau of the Census, 1973), 267. https://www2.census.gov/library/publications/1973/compendia/statab/94ed/1973-05.pdf.

[5] Julie Gilliam, interview by the author, July 26, 2006.

[6] Gene Flores, in discussion with the author (phone) July 15, 2004.

[7] Carl Stone, interview by the author, March 5, 2003.

[8] Oxygen (Nichols, Jean), in discussion with the author (phone), February 23, 2007.

[9] Z'ev, in discussion with the author (phone), July 5, 2004.

[10] Oxygen, Ibid.

[11] Eric Saarinen, in discussion with the author (phone), December 4, 2009.

[12] David Lebrun, in discussion with the author (phone), May 11, 2003.

13 Wavy Gravy. *The Hog Farm and Friends*. New York: Links Books, 1974, 20.
14 Bonds, Ibid.
15 Adam Beckett, "H.R.H. Adam K. Beckett: Itinerary." Progress report to Jim Jordan, his preceptor at Antioch College, 1968. Records received from Antioch College Office of the Registrar with permission from the family.
16 Gravy, Ibid., 86.
17 Ibid., 73.
18 Mark Whitney, interview by the author, April 12, 2003.
19 Vicky Koenig, in discussion with the author (phone), August 24, 2005.
20 Deirdre Beckett, interview by the author, August 17, 2004.
21 John Koenig, in discussion with the author (phone), June 21, 2006.
22 Oxygen, Ibid.
23 Robert Russett, interview of Adam Beckett, November 1974, *Experimental Animation*, 1976, 10.
24 Libby Chaney, in discussion with the author (phone), July 20, 2006.
25 V. Koenig, Ibid.
26 Eve De Bona, email to the author, September 15, 2005.
27 Russett, Ibid., 10.
28 *6shortfilms* can be found at OddBall Films. It was brought to my attention by the cartoonist and filmmaker Matthew Thurber, via email on June 7, 2018.
29 Adam Beckett, First year summary sheet, Antioch College records. Records received from Antioch College Office of the Registrar with permission from the family.

CHAPTER 3

The "Idealistic Young Mystic" at Antioch College

Adam undoubtedly began to work on his ambitious and never-completed *Life in the Atom* while at Antioch. The instructor evaluation for "Making Animated Science Films" read:

> Does beautiful animation! Using lines to make space move in, out, and around itself. Technique well applied to a sex education film. He put a lot of work into his film, doing complete pictures for each frame of film—amounting to a few thousand drawings.[1]

It is interesting that Adam's chosen topic for the animated science film class was sex (Figure 3.1). Perhaps, it was not unusual for a young male who was not yet 20 years old and especially one who had experienced communal living in the late 1960s. While we don't know what images or information the animation included,

FIGURE 3.1 Drawing from sequence of early animation of nude couple, on vertically oriented paper with nail holes, barely visible, at top. (Used with permission from Beckett's family.)

it is highly probable that this is where *Life in the Atom* originated, as an idea, if not as the beginning of the actual animation.

While Adam was a student at Antioch, he drew sequences that were later incorporated into his first film, *Early Animations or*

Quacked Jokes (1970); images from that film also appear in the later *Flesh Flows* (1974). There is evidence that he started *Sausage City,* completed in 1974, while in Ohio. In a letter to Terry Kemper on August 6, 1974, he indicated that he had worked on *Sausage City* "on and off" for 3 to 4 years.[2] He also wrote in a letter to animator Jim Trainor that he started it in 1968.[3]

While there wasn't an official film *program* at Antioch in 1968, there were film classes (and instructors who taught animation, per Adam's class noted previously) and an extremely active film community. Independent films, including works by Stan Brakhage, Norman McLaren, Ken Jacobs, and Stan VanDerBeek, were being screened regularly. Students leaned toward more contemporary art forms, seeking more relevance to the times. They were learning to make films, using equipment, and sometime funding, that the school provided. Projects included frame-by-frame animation, as Adam's student records attest and as confirmed by media artist Shalom Gorewitz, a fellow student.[4] Paul Sharits joined the faculty in 1970 (after Adam had left), initiating a formal film program. In 1973, Tony Conrad took his place, when Sharits moved on to the University of New York in Buffalo. Conrad joined him there a few years later. Students were making films with various approaches, from social documentaries to art films. This is evident in the works of Julia Reichert, who, with Jim Klein, made "Growing Up Female" in the spring of 1970,[5] and of Jay Tuck, who made "The Date," a film exercise, in 1968.[6] They went on to have substantial careers in film and media.

Newly introduced video equipment was available to students. Portable video cameras and decks, while not light or small, made recording and viewing moving images an immediate experience. This new media was being quickly co-opted by young artists, who would form collectives in order to afford equipment. Gorewitz recalls that they had Portapaks and a studio, and they were all experimenting with this new technology.[7] His co-op experience was working with Stan VanDerBeek, so he had access to an even-wider breadth of emerging technology. At that time, VanDerBeek was a research fellow at the Center for Advanced Visual Studies at the Massachusetts Institute of Technology (MIT) and an artist-in-residence at Boston's public television station WGBH.

Art wasn't the only reason that Adam chose Antioch College. A key factor was its reputation as the center of the counterculture in the Midwest. At this time, the schools that attracted high school graduates to more progressive, liberal institutions included Reed College in Portland, Oregon; University of California at Santa Cruz, and Antioch College in Yellow Springs, Ohio. Evergreen State College opened its doors in 1967 and became the newest of the alternative colleges. Adam's sister Morgan attended Evergreen. Like the liberal focus of his earlier education, Antioch also fostered an interdisciplinary approach and placed the responsibility of learning on the individual student, underscoring not just the material to be learned but also the process of learning. According to Gorewitz, there was an introductory class that prepared students for the Antioch mindset. "Antioch... almost indoctrinates you. The first thing you took at Antioch was something they called the 'Unlearning.' You had to go through the Unlearning class as I think it was called. And you had to unlearn all the things you'd learned before in order to be fresh."[8] Renowned filmmaker Bill Brand was also a fellow student and remembers, "Everything was up for question—whether teachers should teach, students knew more than teachers, whether knowledge was attainable—all authority was under question."[9]

Adam's written student self-assessments contain a trace of dismissiveness written in hip jargon. He has an almost arrogant attitude about some of the classes but manages to rein it in and make some positive comments. This is especially noted in a drawing class response, where he criticizes the use of slides for teaching art history. He writes:

> That art history bit, it was a real meaningless thing for me. I did my own art history scene down in the bound art magazine section of the library. I feel a real need to do a

real main number with the teacher and the slides etc. but I admit my own inability to acquiesce to this scene right now. I hope you liked my fictitious Greek Art Test. Art history is a damn sight more than being able to match artist-date to the unknown painting. I look at paintings to get ideas, dig the artist's soul, understand myself.[10]

There is a drawing at the bottom of the page, similar to what later appears in "Early Animations," and at the top left corner, in fancy typeface, there is the phrase "Horse Shit," rubber-stamped twice, upside down. The drawing is his, and the rubber stamp may be as well, or is it an instructor commenting on Adam's methodology and attitude? The instructor has written "Fertile imagination, fecund sensibility."

In the same course evaluation, Adam addresses drawing:

I am the student. Drawing is religion. I worship. A blank piece of paper is like a shot of meth. Any space is an exploding universe which crys [sic] out to be drawn again and again. This quarter many drawings were made by many people. I made some of them; where do they fit in? They fit inside myself.

This quarter I began to stop looking at things in pieces and started looking at each point, angle, tone, in relation to every other point, line. This is the biggest thing ever for me. Suddenly I no longer feel lost inside my drawings but am suddenly in grasp of my eyes. I can encompass.

The effusiveness of the writing makes it difficult to determine if he is being genuine or creating a parody of the evaluation process. Based on Vicky Koenigs's astute recall of Adam drawing constantly, it is most likely genuine. His feedback, here and from another drawing class, notes a change in his approach to drawing and to adding more materials such as charcoal and "differing hardnesses of pencils" to his tool set. His reference to "a shot of meth" raises the question if he is referring to his personal experience with this drug. Methamphetamine was legal in the United States until 1970, available over the counter.

Adam's self-assessment covering the summer and winter quarters of 1968, when he first arrived at Antioch, reveals much more about his personality than what he learned or what was covered in the courses. In a full-typed page addressed to "Mister Jordan," his preceptor (faculty advisor) Jim Jordan, from "H.R.H. Adam K. Beckett," he reviews his first-term experience.

> Well now, Mister Jordan, in the first place I took four courses: Calculus, Drawing, Topology and Set Th. And Ethics. The calculus course got a leetle beet tedius. The ethics course was a leetle beet evanescent. The other two were right up my alley, so to speak, ahem. Now, on to more important matters, here in this paragon of an essay. I did less reading then I feel is necessary to maintain a clear conscience. It is reassuring anyway because it was a lot more than I used to get through at home, that mountainous molehill of books I got through this time around. I have a whole shelf of those I meant to read and 31.72 outstanding debt at the big library over by the tall, gabled gymnasium.[11]

Adam's time at Antioch was productive, even if he had some reservations about the courses. He had found a focus and a direction to channel his energy and drive. He was surrounded by artists, in an environment that would have been familiar to him. His mother recalls that, in a letter, he said, "Well everybody else here is so much like me that I have a lot of friends without even trying."[12] The art students had an abandoned building, an old dorm, to use as studio spaces. As Brand remembers, "It was great. There was this whole hall. And if you were an art student you could get essentially a whole room. In a building that nobody cared what you did to it. It was unsupervised and Adam was down the hall from me."[13]

As early as the summer of 1968, when he was new to campus, Adam includes a comment about his experience in his typed report. "I have a somewhat greater fund of rhetoric to unleash on people, after hearing all the people talk it up thrice a week, up there in the art building." Already, he speaks of the "valuable friendships" that will "always be of great value" and writes that "These people are fine influences on the idealistic young mystic."[14]

Gorewitz also had a studio in the art building and, like Brand, remembers Adam as very creative, somewhat quiet, and in his own world but not shy. He would play guitar and sing funny songs, songs that probably displayed his humor and his tendency to twist words and meanings into whimsy, satire, or irony. Gorewitz also recalls a washboard band that he suspects included Adam. Brand recalls him as sort of a "super hippy" and that he seemed like someone who might be connected to the Hog Farm. Mostly, he worked in his studio and didn't talk about his family or life, which was not uncommon for someone of that age. They were students in the process of becoming.

His teachers' comments in his records recognize Adam's exceptional talent and potential. Jim Jordan writes about Adam's progress in his Drawing and Composition II class:

> Excellent work—Adam has, perhaps, enough talent that it gets in his way. Certainly one of the most imaginative & gifted draughtsman to appear at Antioch in some years. Which is to say that progress for him is proportionately extremely difficult—But the potential for—? "wonder and art" is there![15]

Adam's "fertile imagination" and proclivity toward math were also noted (Figure 3.2). His instructor in Intuitive Topology and Set Theory wrote that Adam's enthusiasm was noted, and while his comments were "often naive, irrelevant and wide of the mark," they were also frequently "remarkable and insightful," summarizing that "He should definitely be encouraged to pursue his interest in

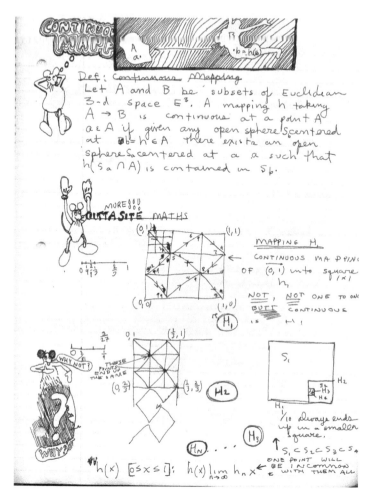

FIGURE 3.2 Page from Adam's "Topology and Set Theory" notebook, with mouse characters illustrating his class notes. (Used with permission from Beckett's family.)

mathematics."[16] While he didn't follow that advice, this proclivity guides his future animation process and his work in visual effects.

While the reviews are positive, Adam was still struggling to come to terms with himself as an artist. This is expressed openly in the aforementioned first-term self-assessment. He writes:

Something about this place saps the energy I need to live up to my self-image as the fantastically productive young artist. I got some things I really like out into the open air. I feel a certain amount of uneasiness over some thoughts I've been having; that, in the long run, concern for some activity like Banking or Arting will render you insensitive to, and incapable of treading, certain religious paths that appear visible in the fog now and again. At least art is a sop for boredom, that at least.[17]

It is interesting that Adam mentions banking and art as two choices that create some anxiety for him. While these two things may seem unrelated, they are directly related to his family, noted patrons of the arts, and specifically his mother's family members, who were bankers. Is he feeling pressure from the Kemper family? His grandfather, James Madison Kemper, who had died in 1965, when they were preparing for their journey to India, was an extremely successful banker, heading Commerce Bank as well as overseeing the William T. Kemper Foundation. His uncle was currently president of Commerce Bank, and undoubtedly cousins would be following the path into banking. It is doubtful that the financial responsibility of being an adult was causing the uneasiness, but it was rather due to the vague question of what career path to pursue as an adult.

His reference to "certain religious paths" is one of the few indications he left in writing that speaks to spirituality, or religious aspiration, perhaps inspired by his time in India and/or with the Hog Farm family. Another indication is when he refers to himself as an "idealistic young mystic," in the self-assessment mentioned previously. Deirdre, while noting that spiritual grounding may have helped him navigate life a bit better, says that he was "spiritual in his own way"[18] and into meditation.

The final paragraph in his first-term self-assessment paints the clearest picture that we have of his time at Antioch and speaks to the ambivalence that he has about being there.

Well, that isn't the whole story. There were untold movies, multi-media Events, Stimulating Disgustions, erotic cafetorium foods, Friendly T-groups and so on. I met some very interesting people, fine women, nice dogs, cats, and faculty, Kampus Kops, Key Officers, and Co-operative Advisors and so on. This place isn't as strange as it might appear at first blush, all long-hairs, druggists, south-hall midnight candles, no grades, midnight movie disturbances etc., aside. It's just a nice quiet place to spend five years getting ready to leave and then not wanting to go, but not being able to stand it here so what do you do. Harsh reality out there calls and grates, oh well, young and flexible...[19]

Clearly, Adam had found a place where there were lots of people like him; however, he is also conflicted about being there. He references "harsh reality" and may have been referring to the social and political landscape that was in chaos, on campus and beyond. Antioch College was populated with students of his age, from various backgrounds, and many were radicalized. The questioning, confrontational environment offered a different type of intensity than his experience with the Hog Farm family, with their pacifist, art-and-music-centered approach to change.

Enrollment in all colleges was rising, owing to changes in educational support in the 1960s, which made the path to college an easier option and open to a more diverse population in terms of gender, race, and economy. The GI Bill made college possible for many returning veterans as well. Young adults also sought college as an alternative to employment, which was becoming increasingly hard to find, and to avoid the draft. Active draft for the Vietnam War ended officially in January of 1973.

Protests and strikes were happening across the country on university campuses, led by this new generation. Dr. Martin Luther King, Jr., had been assassinated earlier in April of 1968, only months before Adam's arrival at Antioch. This would have had a huge impact on that campus. Dr. King's wife, Coretta Scott King, and her older sister, Edythe, had been students at Antioch College, and Dr. King had delivered the 1965 commencement address. Also, in 1965, the college had started the Antioch Program for Interracial Education and received a grant from the Rockefeller Foundation to provide scholarships for minorities, including African American students from urban centers. African American students lobbied for their own dorm and chartered a new African American Studies Institute with courses that only black students could take.[20] The radical atmosphere after Dr. King's murder would also have been fueled by news of race riots across the country, especially in Washington, DC; Baltimore; and Chicago. This undoubtedly impacted Adam, as he wrote in his first-year record that he "... began to get my head together about race relations."[21]

Desegregation and civil rights were just one of the many sources of chaos on campus. The escalating war in Vietnam and the Tet Offensive in January of 1968 caused students to question the education-military connection, to respond with strikes and protests when one was found and to stand up against research being done for the military.[22] Michael Goldfarb had also entered Antioch in 1968 and in 2007 commented on Antioch's impending closing (it closed in 2008 and reopened in 2011), referring to the college as a "sociological petri dish."[23]

> So much of the history of 1968 reflects an America in crisis, but if you were young and idealistic, it was a time of unparalleled excitement. The 2000 students at Antioch, living in a picture-pretty American village, provided a laboratory for various social experiments of the time.
>
> ... Sex, drugs and rock' n' roll became the rule, as you might imagine, and there was enormous peer pressure to be involved in all of them.

As Adam had forewarned in his first-year review, he did not stay. His last course record is from the winter quarter of 1969, which concluded at the end of March of 1970. There was a strike on campus in May of 1970 and on campuses across the United States, sparked by the May 4 Kent State shootings, where protesters were fired on by police, killing four and wounding nine. On May 8, the *New York Times,* in an article titled "College Strife Spreads," reported that 120 universities and colleges were shut down for a day or more.[24]

There are no definite records of Adam reconvening with the Hog Farm after leaving Antioch. The core group of the Hog Farm arrived at Antioch in August of 1970. The buses carried the support team for a traveling music show film project that would eventually appear as "The Medicine Ball Caravan." Their expenses were paid by Warner Bros., and the musicians were flown in to perform. Students at Antioch make an appearance in the film as they clash with the bus residents, seeing them as sell-outs owing to their connection with corporate funding from Warner Bros.[25] In retrospect, Wavy Gravy sees the decision to travel and be filmed as a mistake. His original vision was that the film would be used to gain support for the Earth People's Park project. The journey left them disillusioned, and when they completed the tour in England, they sold their return plane tickets and continued their own brand of concerts and events in England and then on to the continent.[26] The era of the traveling buses was coming to a close, but the Hog Farm family continued—and continues.

Adam's official withdrawal from Antioch is dated June 30, 1970. He, along with his friend Shalom Gorewitz, transferred to a new school near Los Angeles that would open its doors for the first time in the fall of 1970. One wonders if Adam, albeit a born and bred liberal, was looking to retreat from the volatile environment to return to the more familiar West Coast and a school that enabled him to focus solely on his art.

Adam would not be at Antioch College in August of 1970 when the buses arrived. In the 2 years he had been a student there, the optimism of the youth culture had been tempered by a more radical call for change. As demonstrated by the reaction to the Medicine Ball Caravan, young people had become aware that, instead of generating true change, their culture was being co-opted.

In the 3 years since returning from India, Adam had been in motion. His travels with the Hog Farm had showed him a gentler, and sometimes humorous, way of negotiating the world while attempting to promote change. He had experienced collaboration and communal living, with its difficulties, failures, and successes. His art vocabulary was informed by the variety of work he saw beyond the borders of California, art made by his fellow travelers, artists around the country, and his fellow students at Antioch College. While he didn't receive a degree from Antioch, his experience there was critical to his next step. Adam bought his own bus—a new white Volkswagen van—and with his dog, Elvis, headed back to Los Angeles.

BIBLIOGRAPHY

Beckett, Adam. *Letter to Terry Kemper*. Frances Mulhall Achilles Library, Archives. New York: Whitney Museum of American Art, NY. John Hanhardt artist files, Box 3, Adam Beckett folder.

Goldfarb, Michael. "Where the Arts Were Too Liberal," *New York Times*, June 17, 2007. https://www.nytimes.com/2007/06/17/opinion/17goldfarb.html.

Gravy, Wavy. 1974. *The Hog Farm and Friends*. New York: Links Books.

Louima, Gariot P., Tim Anderl and Jill Davis. "There's Something Happening Here: The Class of 1971 and Antioch's Rocky Road to Plurality," *The Antiochian*, Spring/Summer 2013, http://magazine.antiochcollege.org/springsummer-2013/theres-something-happening-here.

McFadden, Robert D. "College Strife Spreads," *New York Times*, May 8, 1970. http://www.nytimes.com/1970/05/08/archives/college-strife-spreads-over-100-schools-closed-and-up-to-350-struck.html?_r=0.

Ouellette, Rick. "The Strange, Forgotten Saga of the Medicine Ball Caravan," *Reel and Rock*, March 3, 2013. https://rickouellettereelandrock.com/2013/03/03/the-strange-forgotten-saga-of-the-medicine-ball-caravan/.

Till, Chris. "Yellow Springs in the '60s and '70s: Medicine Ball Caravan." *Yellow Springs Blog*, November 7, 2011. http://ayellowspringsblog.blogspot.com/2011/11/yellow-springs-in-60s-and-70s-medicine.html.

Whaley, Joseph. 1968. "Antioch Student Protest," *Science* 161(3843), 739. http://science.sciencemag.org/content/161/3843/739.3.

ENDNOTES

1   Instructor's remarks for course "Making Animated Science Films" fall quarter, 1969. Records received from Antioch College Office of the Registrar with permission from the family.

2   Adam Beckett, letter to Terry Kemper, dated August 6, 1974. Frances Mulhall Achilles Library, Archives, Whitney Museum of American Art, NY. John Hanhardt artist files, Box 3, Adam Beckett folder.

3   Beckett, personal letter to Jim Trainor, May 3, 1978.

4   Shalom Gorewitz, in discussion with the author (phone), February 14, 2007.

5   Julia Reichert, "Spotlight on Rebecca Rice Award Winner: Julia Reichert," *The Independent*, A publication for Alumni and Friends, January 6, 2015, Vol. 5, issue 1. Antioch College. http://enews. antiochcollege.org/2015/01/feature/spotlight-rebecca-rice-award-winner-julia-reichert.

6   Jay Tuck, "The Date," 1968. https://www.youtube.com/watch?v=Y-IVh0WUZag.

7   Gorewitz, Ibid.

8   Ibid.

9   Bill Brand, in discussion with the author (phone), July 8, 2004.

10 Beckett, Evaluation Summary for "Drawing and Composition II," winter 1969, Antioch College.

11 Beckett, "H.R.H. Adam K. Beckett: Itinerary." Progress report to James "Jim" Jordan, his preceptor at Antioch College, 1968.

12 Julie Gilliam, interview by the author, July 26, 2006.

13 Brand, Ibid.

14 Beckett, writing his Evaluation Summary for "Drawing and Composition I," Summer, 1968. Antioch College.

15 James Jordan, Instructor's comments on Adam's Evaluation Summary for "Drawing and Composition II," Spring 1969–1970. Antioch College.

16 Mel Steinberg, Instructor's comments, Adam's first-year program evaluation report for "Intuitive Topology and Set Theory," 9-24-68. Antioch College.

17 A. Beckett, "H.R.H. Adam K. Beckett: Itinerary." Progress report to James "Jim" Jordan.

18 Deirdre Beckett, interview by the author, August 17, 2004.

19 Beckett, "H.R.H. Adam K. Beckett: Itinerary."

20 Gariot P. Louima, Tim Anderl and Jill Davis. "There's Something Happening Here: The Class of 1971 and Antioch's Rocky Road to Plurality," *The Antiochian*, Spring/Summer 2013. http://magazine.antiochcollege.org/springsummer-2013/ theres-something-happening-here.

21 Beckett, First-year program activities, Preceptor's Summary page 3. Antioch College.

22 Joseph Whaley, "Antioch Student Protest," Letter to the Editor, *Science*. Vol. 161, Issue 3843, 739. American Association for the Advancement of Science. August 23, 1968. http://science.sciencemag.org/content/161/3843/739.3. Whaley was a student who participated in group to protest defense research at Antioch.

23 Goldfarb, Michael, "Where the Arts Were Too Liberal," *New York Times*, June 17, 2007. https://www.nytimes.com/2007/06/17/ opinion/17goldfarb.html.

24 Robert D. McFadden, "College Strife Spreads," *New York Times*, May 8, 1970, 1. http://www.nytimes.com/1970/05/08/archives/ college-strife-spreads-over-100-schools-closed-and-up-to-350-struck.html?_r=0.

25 Rick Ouellette, "The Strange, Forgotten Saga of the Medicine Ball Caravan," *Reel and Rock*, March 3, 2013. https://rickouellettereelandrock.com/2013/03/03/the-strange-forgotten-saga-of-the-medicine-ball-caravan/comment-page-1/. Also see Chris Till, "Yellow Springs in the '60s and '70s: Medicine Ball Caravan," *Yellow Springs Blog*, November 7, 2011. http://ayellowspringsblog.blogspot.com/2011/11/yellow-springs-in-60s-and-70s-medicine.html.

26 Wavy Gravy, *The Hog Farm and Friends*. New York: Links Books, 1974, 131.

CHAPTER 4

Two Letters and a New School

A DAM RETURNED TO LOS Angeles in the summer of 1970 to join the inaugural class of the newly formed CalArts. Classes would not begin until October, and the facilities were not ready. He arrived with drawings for an animation and needed a place to shoot, so he temporarily moved into a communal house on Heliotrope, shared by Eric Saarinen, Joan Churchill, and a lively community of artists experimenting with film.[1] Saarinen and Churchill were students at the University of California, Los Angeles. Saarinen was on his way to becoming an award-winning director of documentary films and commercials. Churchill became an acclaimed cinematographer and director, known for her documentary films. (Saarinen's father was the renowned architect Eero Saarinen.)

Saarinen recalls that Adam retreated to his room with a light, a Bolex camera, and a collection of drawings and stayed there for what seemed like 4 days. The result was *Early Animations or Quacked Jokes*, a valuable document of his early experimentation with materials, timing, and techniques. We witness Adam learning to animate, through this 12-minute collection of exercises and studies. The title, *Early Animations,* foreshadowed the animations that were to come; three projects borrowed segments from this first exploration.

There are eight distinct segments, including a humorous opening that precedes the title. It is silent, and there are no apparent edits; his mistakes and retakes are all there. His primary method is hand-drawn metamorphosing of forms and figures, a native straight-ahead animation technique (as opposed to using keyframes and in-betweens). Two sections of this early film include the first known examples of the evolving cycle technique he developed. He created a simple animation cycle then added to the drawings each time they repeated under the camera. In this way, the single image—and the animation—would grow in complexity, building on the original cycle.

His humor and his exploration of timing and sequencing are apparent immediately in the opening of the film. His pseudonym "Algernon Picayune" appears in a playful, meandering moment that ends abruptly, replaced with "HELP!!! I GOT THE BRAIN MAGGOTS." The words morph into squiggling lines, reform, and repeat with variations in timing, so that the squiggles appear to change, as their motion ping-pongs forward and backward. The surface that he was shooting on is visible at the edges of the frame and may be a wooden floor, or a board with nails, as he was using nail-punched paper. (This is confirmed by drawings that were found.)

The "brain maggots" sequence ends abruptly, replaced by "EARLY ANIMATIONS" that is animated in several different ways. The second part of his title, "OR QUACKED JOKES," appears to be moving significantly smoother than the first part. The title transforms into the body of the animation, the lines forming a nude female that lacks arms or a head. She constantly mutates, as her neck stretches out to engulf a cloud. Organic abstractions extend from where her head would be; one tubular form curves down to enter her vagina. A circle appears, through which the flowing, organic forms exit the scene, as the remaining female morphs to completion, still without arms or a face but now having three breasts.

This abstracted female segment parallels a section of Adam's *Flesh Flows*. There, 4 years later, the timing is faster and the animated motion is smoother. While the image is flipped and framed differently, with no part of the woman's figure cropped, these two films clearly use the same drawings.

The use of images of the naked body, particularly the female body, was well established in the underground comix scene that emerged in the late 1960s, and was a natural subject of interest for a 20-year-old heterosexual male navigating the space between adolescence and adulthood. In Adam's work, the body has a surreal, symbolic presence. In the next segment, featuring a nude male and female couple, a comic word bubble appears, announcing "a brief word from our sponsor." A cartoon version of Adam appears. He is depicted fairly simply, with shoulder-length hair, wearing a striped shirt, at an animation desk, with pen in hand (Figure 4.1). This scene is enclosed in a rectangle, referencing a comic panel. The figure turns toward the audience and, via word balloon, says "WE'RE ALL IN THIS TOGETHER." A large finger appears between his legs, obviously referencing an erection, which secretes a text balloon from its tip, saying "YES." The animator's words disintegrate and fall on the desk, and the disjointed lines suggest hairs of the female pubis.

Another nude female appears in a later section that quite possibly came from his sex education animation that was mentioned in his records from Antioch. She is drawn in the simple style of the female figure appearing in his comic drawings from that time and in early segments of *Life in the Atom,* which he had already begun. Here unfolds a psychedelic reflection of the political climate. The woman transforms from a comical floating head to a full figure that is impregnated by a large undefined phallic form that enters from the bottom of the screen. She rubs her pregnant belly and then gives birth to an orb that she takes and places on her shoulders to replace her head that had disappeared. Her body is absorbed into the rotating orb, the Earth, on which the words

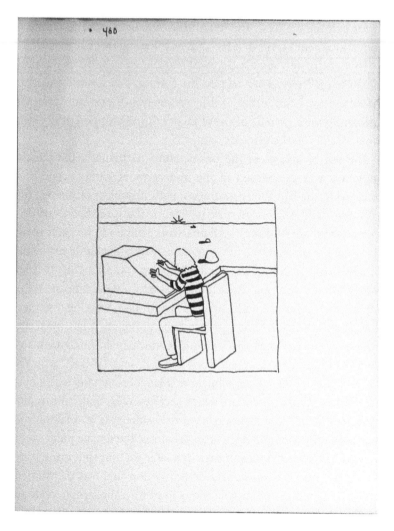

FIGURE 4.1 Self-reference as an animator in *Early Animations*. (Used with permission from Beckett's family.)

"EARTH" and "ABIDES" appear, followed by a "?" a mushroom cloud erupts from the top, and a single eye appears on the globe. This segment reflects the time in which it was created; the Cold War was keenly felt, and the fear of nuclear destruction was palatable.

Abruptly, the next segment begins with a black-and-white photograph of President Richard Nixon with his wife, Pat. Adam drew on a transparent overlay, causing Nixon to grow an impressive wild beard and bush of hair. Their photograph is replaced by the nude torso of a woman, with her hand over her pubic area. Political jabs appeared in numerous Adam's drawings. It was a time of irreverence; the mighty had fallen, and the curtain had been pulled aside to reveal flawed humans in seats of power. Authority was a target for ridicule, including the institution built by Disney. One of Adam's comics is of a character modeled after Scrooge McDuck, with top hat and cane, standing next to a sign advertising "Vista Valencia." He's pointing at a cube-shaped building that sits on top of a hill, with a large "$" on it and "C.I.A III" in tiny letters, referencing the California Institute for the Arts (Figure 4.2). The artist's signature is that of Bebe Rebozo, a noted Florida banker and confidant of Nixon.

FIGURE 4.2 Comic with a critical eye on CalArts, signed as Bebe Rebozo. (Used with permission from Beckett's family.)

The final section is an evolving cyclical sequence of a geometric, abstract form that becomes more complex with each repetition of the cycle. A nearly identical version of this appears in *The Letter,* which he was working on around the same time; this section may have been the springboard to that collaboration between Adam and James Gore. A close, frame by frame analysis comparing the two animations on the computer confirms that the same drawings are used; however, the timing doesn't match, indicating that frames were added or subtracted. In *The Letter,* the size of the shape in the frame differs, is slightly rotated, and is reversed horizontally. The color is inverted, with the drawing being a pale blue on a medium blue background. These shifts suggest the use of the optical printer or some process of re-photographing the projected animation during his first or second term at CalArts, when he had access to equipment and instruction.

When Adam appeared on campus that summer, hoping to be able to work, Jules Engel was there, assisting with application review. He recalls, "... he was asking me, can I start to work tomorrow, and I said, we have a month left, we're not ready with anything. And I remember it was a hot sunny day and he had all of his animation papers... he was ready to shoot!"[2] Engel, who had projected cartoons at Adam's birthday party many years earlier, was there to head the Film Graphics area that would become the Experimental Animation program, a pivotal program in American independent animation.

This new institution was far removed from Antioch College, geographically and in spirit. The CalArts that Adam first arrived at was temporarily located in Villa Cabrini Academy, a former private Catholic school for girls located just outside of Burbank. (It's now Woodbury University.) The permanent campus in Valencia was still under construction and opened on November 1, 1971, 10 years after the incorporation of CalArts. Founded and funded by Disney, it was created from the merger of the Chouinard School of Art and the Los Angeles Conservatory of Music. Only a few of the art instructors from Chouinard would make their way onto the art faculty of CalArts. Emerson Woelffer and Matsumi (Mike) Kanemitsu made the transition; both had their work hanging in Julie's home.

CalArts was looking to other experiments happening in higher education, including the influential, but short-lived, Black Mountain College. They sought faculty who were working artists, brought in to teach the students by example. Paul Brach was hired to head the art school. He and his wife, Miriam Schapiro, were established artists who'd left the New York art world for the West Coast. In discussing his reasons for taking on the task at this new institution, Brach stated:

> What really knocked me out was that the makers of *Mary Poppins* are inadvertently funding something that's going to make *Easy Rider*. ... the whole level of large ironic culture joke in Cal Arts is fascinating. I mean, the school is nowhere, nowhere in these beautiful hills.[3]

Many of the artists that Brach hired were also from the East Coast and participants in the Fluxus movement. Alison Knowles was brought onboard to set up and run the print shop. She recalls their transition. "We were from the east, we were doing experimental work of various types. I was doing experimental works in printing and performance and Nam June was into video and Jim Tenney was into sound and kind of the legacy of Cage and bringing that to CalArts."[4]

Mel Powell, a leading composer who had studied under Paul Hindemith, was the dean of the music school. The music composition department was led by Associate Dean Morton Subotnick, one of the founders of the San Francisco Tape Music Center and a pioneer in electronic compositions using manipulated tape and other electronic media. Tenney brought his work in electronic and computer music. There was also a strong world music program, which attracted artists such as Ravi Shankar. Music students had a wide spectrum of choices—from analog synthesizers to Gamelan instruments.

The art school included a Critical Studies area, led by Allan Kaprow, which included instructors Dick Higgins, writer and artist, and Emmett Williams, the poet, all connected to Fluxus. Nam June Paik, who was already a star in the art world, was there with the engineer Shuya Abe, building their video synthesizer. Gene Youngblood taught film theory; his class was "Expanded Cinema," also the title of his groundbreaking book that was published in that same year.

The "fluid state" felt at the genesis was communicated in the letter of admission, dated March 4, 1970, that Adam received from Alexander (Sandy) Mackendrick, dean of the school of film:

> Fortunately, the section we're calling Film Graphics (which includes animation and many other things) is in better shape than some as regards planning our equipment resources and recruiting faculty... we're at a stage where students' comment can have some influence. I'd like to explain some of the things we have in mind and hear your views.[5]

In the film school, instructors included live action filmmakers Kris Malkiewicz and Don Levy, teaching cinematography courses. Pat O'Neill was an emerging West Coast experimental filmmaker using multiple-image work and a novel approach to filmmaking; he was recruited to teach optical printing, a technology that Adam would embrace. Engel, as noted, was in charge of the Film Graphics area, hired for his experience in the animation industry and as an independent artist. Engel had a keen sense of color and design, evident in his innovative work across various practices.

Like Adam's previous educational environments—with the exception of the Jesuit school in India and his short stint in a public school—CalArts was liberal. Its early years were somewhat of an experiment. O'Neill recalled, "That first year, especially when they were in Villa Cabrini, was sort of wonderful because the architectural space didn't dictate that people were off by themselves, they were all crossing over one another. Nobody would know necessarily where somebody was from, and there these conversations would happen and it seemed like 'oh, this is good and this probably is going to get better.'"[6]

Barry Schrader was finishing his master of fine arts degree in the music school and remembers the first year as one of the most unique experiences in his life, as it was a "study in anarchy."

> We were coming off of the highs of the 60s countercultural and experimental art movement(s) and there was a great deal of activity, but little structure.... We were provided with tools and left to our own devices to create and do what we wanted. It was sort of a giant arts laboratory. I taught a class on the Buchla 100 that began at midnight, which, at the time, didn't seem all that unusual as there was activity going on 24 hours a day. It truly was a community of artists and we all seemed part of a huge extended family.[7]

Just over a week after Adam turned 20 years old, the community that was flourishing at the Villa Cabrini campus was disrupted in the middle of its second term. On February 9, the San Fernando—or Sylmar—earthquake struck with a magnitude of 6.6; its center was located between the temporary campus and the Valencia campus, which was under construction.

CalArts became a divided entity as they struggled to keep classes going. Some areas moved to Valencia ahead of the rest of the school and before facilities were ready to open. When the campus finally moved to Valencia, the communal unity was changed owing to the physical space, but the alternative structure of the curriculum remained intact. There were no grades. Between the years 1970 and 1975, the students wrote their own record, with an occasional comment from an instructor. Their records documented what class was taken and sometimes had a description or a note about what the student worked on. Each student was assigned a mentor, and Adam's mentor was Engel.

The distinction between a student and a teacher was not always clear. A few students taught courses, based on their unique expertise or interests. Gorewitz, who was there to complete his final undergraduate year, taught "Experimental Learning II—Beatnik Literature." Adam described the class in his record. "This was an ongoing course consisting of reading beatnik literature and meeting at irregular intervals to discuss same while participating in various related activities such as hikes, lunch, etc."[8]

In the first 2 years in particular, there was an atmosphere of events and art happening all the time, anywhere. To Adam, who had grown up around art and artists (remember the totem pole) and had participated in the artistic shenanigans of the Hog Farm, this was familiar ground. As O'Neill recalled, "Art and life were really passing through one another in a way that it never did again there."[9] Life and learning were spontaneous, and irregular. Gorewitz described the early environment noting that when something occurred, such as Ravi Shankar performing, "the whole campus would pretty much gather. And then the rest of the time everyone was just sort of doing their own thing, their work."[10]

Alison Knowles's "House of Dust," based on a computer-generated poem that she had created in 1967 with the help of James Tenney, was brought to campus. Knowles explained:

> This "House of Dust," which looked quite a lot like an amoeboid shape, it was about six feet high, and fifteen feet long and there were two of them. And I put them on the hill there, and we could... meet there, we could go inside and talk about performance and stuff that we would be doing on certain holidays or we could invent a holiday.[11]

In the second academic year, Judy Chicago was hired, who joined Miriam Shapiro in leading the Feminist Art courses, as well as in the forming of the Feminist Art Project and the Womanhouse space in Los Angeles. The presence of these voices on campus is interesting when considering Adam's varied depictions of the female form in his drawing and future films, *Life in the Atom* and

Flesh Flows. Gorewitz, who had known Adam at Antioch, didn't see him much at CalArts, even though it was a small campus and Adam was a hard person to miss. Adam disappeared into the Film Graphics program. His focus was now on animation, and that meant hours of drawing and working under the camera.

Another student, Michael Scroggins, had worked extensively as a light show artist before coming to CalArts, and knew members of the Hog Farm family. He remembers the first time he met Adam. "The very first day of school, a group of us was standing around and there is this big tall guy with this short haircut and this long thin braid, very long, maybe three feet long... So I met Adam and we struck it off and said oh yeah, he knew the Hog Farm and the people. The whole light show was connected initially with the Hog Farm."[12]

The list of instructors for Adam's first-term classes reads like a who's who of artists and theorists. He took Film Graphics with Jules Engel and Jim Fletcher, Cinematography with Don Levy, and Optical Effects with O'Neill. He also took two classes in the Critical Studies area: Silk Screen with Alison Knowles and Video Workshop with Nam June Paik. Engel's class, while called "Film Graphics," included screenings and discussion of animated, as well as live action, films. Works by Oskar Fischinger, which Adam had seen in his childhood, were included, as was the work of Len Lye, Harry Smith, Norman McLaren, and avant-garde filmmaker Maya Deren.

Adam took two terms of Expanded Cinema with Gene Youngblood. Gorewitz recounts that they watched 100 films—and videos—in Youngblood's class. The artists discussed in his book, and likely in class, included a variety of artists such as Jordan Belson, Stan Brakhage, Andy Warhol, John Whitney, Sr., and Michael Snow. The ideas articulated in Youngblood's book were groundbreaking and prescient. Their discussions would have covered television, emerging video, and computer technologies as new forms, offering new opportunities for content and structure. His theoretical formulations of "synaesthetic cinema" and syncretic content were potent ideas for Adam's work. In his preface to *Expanded Cinema,* Youngblood writes:

> When we say expanded cinema we actually mean expanded consciousness. Expanded cinema does not mean computer films, video phosphors, atomic light, or spherical projections. Expanded cinema isn't a movie at all: like life it's a process of becoming, man's ongoing historical drive to manifest his consciousness outside of his mind, in front of his eyes. One no longer can specialize in a single discipline and hope truthfully to express a clear picture of its relationships in the environment. This is especially true in the case of the intermedia network of cinema and television, which now functions as nothing less than the nervous system of mankind.[13]

As is apparent, Youngblood had an overarching grasp of the growing impact of moving image media and the potential experiences offered in emerging technologies. He brought that perspective and knowledge to CalArts.

Video experiments and new visual and sonic forms were being explored in the studio. Scroggins, Gorewitz, and Adam took Paik's video course. Gorewitz remembers that Paik, while not on campus regularly, was a magnetic personality and that the students loved him. Scroggins describes his experience:

> Paik and Shuya Abe were building this video synthesizer. It took the better part of the semester to get the thing running. And Nam June was holding up tin foil and blinking Christmas lights in front of this amazing image generator and saying "ahhh beauteous, beauteous" and the students were scratching their heads like "what's this, it's so cheesy" and of course Nam June was trying to say it's all cheesy, in his Fluxus way. I got it right away. I thought "this is pretty funny."[14]

The processing of the image on the video synthesizer and the electronic feedback of video were critical to Adam's developing visual language and engaged his engineering sensibility in terms of feedback loops and taking an input through various processes, changing the signal. While he remained focused on hand-drawn animation, this new media became part of his repertoire.

Adam's CalArts records have few comments from him or his instructors. The Expanded Cinema class description is "Film screening of 'underground' films and some discussion." While the records aren't effusive, his prolific drawing and abundant film elements demonstrate that he was definitely on fertile ground. The equipment that he needed was there, as was the dedicated time for his work. In the interview with Russett, several years later, Adam commented on the impact of working in an educational environment, reflecting the early philosophy behind CalArts.

> Besides those impalpable qualities of talent and drive, otherwise known as inspiration and perspiration, there is one thing that every artist must have, that is, a great deal of free and uninterrupted working time. Schools can help the student-artist in this regard by providing 24-hour access to facilities, flexible mandatory requirements, adequate living arrangements, and other similar kinds of conveniences. The teaching is probably best done by people who themselves are professional artists and who are so wrapped up in their own work that they don't have time to interfere too much in the activities of students. They should be there primarily as examples of what it is to be a working artist in the field of animation. In a medium like animation, which is so dependent on the technology, the best possible equipment and facilities are, of course, also extremely helpful. As far as I can see, it is a matter of the most extraordinary circumstances and luck, when an individual manages to emerge from the educational system with the autonomy of spirit and knowledge needed for him to be an artist. Too much direction is probably more harmful than too little.[15]

With the small collective of Film Graphics students, he spent hours drawing and shooting on the animation camera and optical printer. Jules Engel, in his interview with Helder Sun and Wade Ivy, recalled that Adam hadn't had much drawing, being from math (which wasn't the case). Perhaps Engel was influenced by Adam's concerns about his ability to draw, as his mother said that he didn't feel that he drew well and therefore gravitated to animation. The archive of his numerous drawings tells a different story, as does the instructor remarks from Mike Kanemitsu's class, Drawing and Draftsmanship, which Adam described in his records as a "very intense figure drawing course." Kanemitsu wrote: "Adam is the most serious and hard-working student I have in this class. His drawing excites me every time he touches the paper. Also his animated film is the most beautiful and original. He is an artist. Cal Arts should be very proud of him."[16]

The films that Kanemitsu would have seen are the many loops that Adam had created during his independent project courses, and perhaps, pieces of *Dear Janice,* which he was working on during this term, November 1971 through January 2, 1972. Undoubtedly, *The Letter* had also made an impact on campus.

Printmaking is pivotal to Adam's work in terms of the process and attention to detail. He first did printmaking in high school and continued it at Antioch, focusing on intaglio (Figure 4.3) with some silk-screen work. Then, he took silk-screen printing with Knowles at CalArts. Numerous prints, in various stages of completion, are among the artwork that he left behind. There is a silk-screened book series, skillfully bound to replicate a library book with the call numbers FUCK, containing handwritten indecipherable words and sexual imagery. There is an exquisite print that links Adam's rapidograph drawings, surreal sexual tableaux, and future animations. It is signed Oscar McSpheroid, 1942. There are three distinguishable female characters and a male satyr. Bodies morph and merge in detailed organic forms, set in an abstracted space (Figure 4.4).

In this same term, Adam took a Language Happenings course with the Fluxus poet Emmett Williams. Adam's comments on the class are, "This is a one-to-one informal seminar which met

FIGURE 4.3   Intaglio print from Antioch; notice the concentric lines defining the female form. (Used with permission from Beckett's family.)

whenever we encountered each other. I did some animated typography which is why I was in the class." Williams included a comment on the record: "Adam's work is innovative and I'll do my best to get his work shown at exhibitions of visual poetry this year."

O'Neill taught Adam for five terms. In Adam's course record for the Advanced Optical Printing class of January 1972, O'Neill wrote:

FIGURE 4.4 The "Oscar McSpheroid" silk screen showcases Adam's printmaking, a process that links to the complexity, planning, and repetition of animation. (Used with permission from Beckett's family.)

Adam surfaced from time to time with incredible pieces of film—animated "endless loops" and color mutations of these done on the printer. We have made tentative steps toward collaborating on some short pieces passing the results back and forth. Adam's direction is very strong and he is entirely committed and self-motivated.[17]

This assessment reflects Adam's tendency to work independently and obsessively. It also demonstrates the high regard that O'Neill had for him, as they were considering collaborating. O'Neill's work from that period made use of live action footage, layered and restructured via the optical printer. Adam used a film that he shot while walking in the canyons near his house to matte into the center of the animated, cycling world of the final segment of *Dear Janice,* perhaps as an exercise in process. The film was completed for an independent project in the second term of 1972, which ended on March 31.

Adam's quiet, removed demeanor seems to have been left at Antioch. From this time period, he was still regarded as a lone agent but more confident and to some, intimidating, owing to his straightforward manner and his large presence, physically and otherwise. Although Adam could still be described as someone apart, who had difficulty in navigating the world on other people's terms, his first years at CalArts were seemingly happy and were obviously productive. He was consistently seen by his friends and colleagues as an incredibly smart person: someone who read voraciously and processed what he read in amazing ways.

He rented a house in Val Verde, which was, at that time, a poor, mostly black working-class and farming neighborhood near Valencia. Even though off campus, he spent many nights—and days—in the studios. He quickly grasped the system devised for equipment checkout and sign up. The animation camera and optical printer had to be reserved for use and was available for 24-hour access. Loring Doyle remembers trying to get there early, before Adam, as he, like many others, preferred the night shift. "He was just so dedicated to his art. That was his driving force.... when we used to have to sign up for the Oxberry, he would be the first one who had... stayed up all night to be there when the cage opened in the morning to sign up for his time. He'd be there from midnight 'til eight in the morning or whatever he could get, hour-wise."[18] Chris Casady, who was a year behind Adam, also remembers that Adam had "providence over the equipment." He could be intimidating to the other students and was definitely a presence—the "big man on campus" within the film school.[19]

Casady had heard of Adam even before coming to CalArts, owing to a flyer that had caught his attention at Cartoon Colour, an animation supply store located in Culver City. Adam had posted the flyer in search of other animators to contribute to a chain-letter animation. The idea of collaboration was mentioned in his records, in which he and O'Neill considered collaborating, and in two other independent studies. In term two, January and February of 1971, it is noted in his records that he "manufactured 25 portable animation boards in the workshop for an animated chain letter project." Some of these animation boards may have been taken to the Junior Art Center at Barnsdall, as Libby Chaney, who taught there, recalled that he brought over little stands that he had made for them to use.[20]

In another independent study, in term three (March and April of 1971), he mentions an "animated chain letter" along with loops and "various under-the-camera animations." There are two known animation projects that were collaborative: *The Letter* with James Gore and *Every Body,* with Kathy Rose. However, Rose didn't arrive at CalArts until later, in the fall of 1972. He may have been shooting *The Letter*; however, it screened at Annecy in June 1971, which leaves a close window for submission.

Adam's work on *The Letter* started after his return to Los Angeles and coincided with his shooting of *Early Animations.* James Gore, his collaborator, had left Los Angeles and was living on the Monterey peninsula with his wife, Eve De Bona, and a newborn daughter, Ariel, born in late June of 1970. The process of collaboration was described by De Bona as a sort of exquisite corpse, with images sent by mail.[21] They continued the animation from where the other stopped, echoing and playing off of each other's drawings.

In the simplest sense, it is an animation of someone struggling to express their thoughts in a letter, finally achieving that task and sending it off. The form reflects their process, both in terms of contemplation and in the exchange of images via the postal system. The contemplative struggle to write, and to create, is expressed as the character's head transforms into a variety of human and/or animal personas. The scribbled text eventually becomes a changing series of images as well.

The assumption has been that Adam's contribution was the "geometrical sequence,"[22] an abstracted envelope-like shape that first appeared in *Early Animations*. This is understandable, as that segment differs from the other sections of the film in its color and subject, leading to the assumption that it was a singular contribution by Adam. Researching his work, and Gore's, it is clear that this was more collaborative, a back and forth, as described by De Bona.

In *The Letter,* there are two distinct image segments that alternate: one primarily of black-and-white drawings and the second rendered with color markers. Studying the film and other drawings of characters by Adam, it is likely that he contributed the color marker segments. A stack of these drawings was found in his materials. The character rendered in color markers is slightly different, with a key indicator of authorship being the hands. Those in the color marker sections resemble hands that appear in other Adam drawings and, specifically, those of the strange man that enters the frame toward the end of Adam's later film *Sausage City*. The striped clothing demonstrates the tendency for obsessive doodling or pattern making present in Adam's drawings and also appears in other drawings, such as his self-portrait in *Early Animations*. The stark black-line drawings (with minimal color) contort more grotesquely; these fantastic faces have a distinct kinship with Gore's black-and-white surreal faces and figures from his *Dream of the Sphinx*. Gore's drawings of faces that appear on the page in *The Letter* are used again as an uninterrupted sequence, removed from the context of a letter, in *6shortfilms,* by Gore, dated 1973. The grotesque, unstable persona that Gore depicts references his direct knowledge of Art Brut works, especially that of the artist Jean Dubuffet, from when Gore lived in Vence, in the south of France.[23] (This would have been in the 1960s.)

Adam, as seen in *Early Animations,* used nails on a board to register his drawings in his earliest work. While it had been assumed that Adam got the idea from Gore to use this method to register his work, it may be the opposite. Gore was seen doing that later, when he was on campus, as reported by David Wilson, a student at that time.[24] According to Gore's daughter, Ariel, his drawings for *Dream of the Sphinx* and *The Letter* have no registration holes—nail or otherwise. *Dream of the Sphinx*, shot in a small studio in Gore's backyard, may have been "underlit" by taping the images to a window. Adam's drawings for *The Letter* used nail holes for registration on letter-sized paper. One of the drawings in the archive has a cutout area where the letter appears, so that drawings could be inserted, or "matted in," underneath while shooting (Figure 4.5).

The Letter was selected to screen in the category referred to in their archive as "Graduation Films" in the eighth Annecy International Film festival. Caroline Leaf's *Sand or Peter and the Wolf,* made while at Harvard University (then Radcliff), was also included in that category. A review in *Graphis* gave considerable notice to *The Letter,* publishing three still images and reporting that the film had won second prize in its category.[25] It is referred to as *La Lettre;* the title appearing on the film that was restored is *Une Lettre à un Ami.*

Gore had also submitted *Dream of the Sphinx,* and it won Honorable Mention in the official Annecy Festival. There were six stills from that film in *Graphis*, with Weinstock, the reviewer,

FIGURE 4.5   Drawing from *The Letter*, with cutout for images to be inserted. (Used with permission from Beckett's family.)

stating that Gore was "one of the discoveries of the Annecy Festival." They also reported that he was "a painter and draughts-man from California Institute of the Arts and at present living in France." Gore was never enrolled as a student at CalArts but did sit in on Engel's classes, and when he was there, it was usually with Adam. This was after Annecy; Gore recalls that he first met Engel at Annecy. Gore was back in France, endeavoring to live abroad with his family, at the time of the festival.

The success of *The Letter* at Annecy would have been impres-sive and undoubtedly buoyed Adam's confidence and status as he entered his senior year in the winter of 1971. He was deeply involved in shooting *Dear Janice,* another animated letter of sorts. He finished it in late spring of 1972, and it was his first solo effort to screen in public.

Dear Janice is a complexly animated, affectionate, and short written message: "Dear Janice, May this sight find you well, I just wanted to say hello. Love, Adam." The words, with shapes and forms, develop throughout 7 minutes of an evolving, mesmerizing, and additive cycle. The camera, too, is on a circular, cyclical path, following the evolution. Once the message is completed, the undulating field of metamorphosing graphics grows in complexity for another 9 minutes, giving testimony to a complicated, whimsical, and obsessive world. It is the most personal of his films, in that it reveals tenderness and a playful flirtation. It also directly references his life, through his words and the live footage that is matted into the later portion of the film. The identity of Janice is unknown; however, clearly, this was inspired by an amorous and unrequited attraction.

Dear Janice is a critical work in the development of Adam's endless, evolving cycle technique, his signature contribution to animation. The cycle is a basic tool of animation, as viewed on circular optical toys that predate cinema, such as the zoetrope and praxinoscope. When animations migrated to film, the cycle made repeated movements—such as the motion of legs when walking—more efficient to create. The first complete sequence of movements was drawn, and those drawings reused as the walk was shot on film, negating the need for redundant drawings. A cycle could also be used as a film loop, a piece of film created to be projected continuously, the beginning and end spliced together. Adam made numerous film loops during his time at CalArts, as did his peers.

Adam approached the cycle as the foundation, a recursive element that would develop continuously to create a complex whole. For *Dear Janice*, he used a base cycle of 24 drawings that animated to form the letter "D" of the word "DEAR" when shot under the camera.[26] Once he shot drawing 24, he returned to number 1 and added to the drawing, so that an "E" begins to appear, repeating this cyclical additive process as the other letters, and shapes, emerge. The original 24 images are completely transformed at the end, each is now covered with shapes and colors. In this way, he created an undulating mass of familiar visual phrases, as the cycles made an extraordinary number of passes under the camera. He was working on an Oxberry animation stand, which offered opportunities for him to innovate and orchestrate while shooting. Continuously morphing text and colorful shapes cavort on a circular path, with the text moving counterclockwise, as do some of the shapes. Other shapes counter the movement, moving clockwise, adding to the harmonious cacophony, a complex, elaborate experience for "Janice" and the viewer. Watching the film makes it apparent that he had an extraordinary capability to plan and keep track of movement and image, with indefatigable focus.

Metamorphosing forms is a mainstay of Adam's work, achieved through his evolving cycle and transmutation of his images on the optical printer. The morph, while basic in concept and execution, holds critical potential for expression and meaning. What is unique, and confounding, about Adam's morphing cycles is that the evolution never reaches completion; the forms morph but return to their original state, only to repeat their evolutionary journey many times more.

The shapes and forms of *Dear Janice,* as they cavort around the central space, are the distracted and perhaps disconcerted contemplation of a person who is immersed in the graphic language of the time, while pondering the possible aspects of a relationship that doesn't transpire. Hearts disappear into holes and re-emerge, forming disembodied breasts, and unfolding paths continue to unfold, ad infinitum.

To add to the complexity and structure of the overall piece, he moved the camera closer to the image plane to focus on areas within the complex whole. At one moment, a single form is so close—as if our face is near the paper—that the focus cannot hold. The drawing was moved carefully in calculated increments on the Oxberry animation stand, giving the impression that the camera was following the frolicking shapes as they journeyed along their circular path, adding to the complex illusion of an endless world, or whirl, of rhythmic forms. Through the calculated movements of the camera and image, we get the effect of edits, as if we are looking at a different segment of animation, and not just a portion of the whole.

The complexity of thinking, as he worked out the growing controlled chaotic swarm of images, speaks to his mathematical talent and his obsessive nature. It also points to the impending intersection of old and new as the idea of recursive entities, and the underlying principle of "repeat/while" plays an integral role in the parallel language of computer programming.

It is not coincidental that Adam selected a musical score of several J.S. Bach compositions. The actual compositions are hard to pin down, being played on single instruments and by emerging (now established) musicians. (The magnetic track for the Brandenburg Concerto #5 was among the film elements in the Adam inventory.) His use of the repetitive and evolving loop has a close association with the fugue in music composition, a form that Bach mastered. The fugue, in layman's terms, has a subject that is introduced at the beginning, repeated with change, and woven through in various "voices" to build the whole. Complexity builds while harmony is formed, and the subject remains distinguishable. In *Dear Janice,* Adam creates a layered and repeating visual fugue, driven by several of Bach's musical scores. The various J.S. Bach's compositions begin on guitar (by Eric Jones), then piano (by Emily Wong), and then harpsichord (by Barbara Cadranel). The structure of the film is supported by changes in the sound score, which also evolves, becoming denser as the piece progresses, with the more saturated tones of the harpsichord accompanying more than half of the film.

A discussion of the fugue by the Anteater, Tortoise, and Achilles in *Godel, Escher, Bach: an Eternal Golden Braid* gives some insight to *Dear Janice* as well. Anteater notes that "Fugues have that interesting property, that each of their voices [each visual path within the animation] is a piece of music in itself; and thus a fugue might be thought of as a collection of several distinct pieces of music, all based one single theme, all played simultaneously."[27] In watching the animation, there is the experience of watching the whole and then shifting to follow the development of a particular part, going from the larger to the more singular unit. This syncretic experience of the film is addressed in a chapter of Youngblood's text. As he noted, "… when the 'content' of the message is the relationship between its parts, and when structure and content are synonymous, all elements are equally significant."[28] This undoubtedly resonated with Adam. His work is the constantly metamorphosing whole made of the ever-evolving parts.

Dear Janice is drawn in the graphic arts style echoed in various drawings by Adam and in the colorful style of the late 1960s and early 1970s. The "D" of "DEAR" morphs from a heart, and a heart emerges from the "e" of Janice," as befits a love letter. This heart travels upward, as it changes into lips. Then, this heart disappears in a hole and exits as a new shape that becomes very definite large breasts (Figure 4.6). Adam used a variety of drawing styles and media, shading some forms completely, while cross-hatching others with a marker, and some forms appear to be made from pastel or Conté crayon. There is a variety of abstract forms from an

FIGURE 4.6 Frame from *Dear Janice* illustrating the beginning circular path of the evolving images. (Used with permission from the iotaCenter.)

FIGURE 4.7 Frame from *Dear Janice* showing a variety in shading and media, as "Love Adam" emerges. (Used with permission from the iotaCenter.)

unfolding, polygonal path, ribbons of color, and orange-yellow rounded shapes (Figure 4.7).

O'Neill attested to the influence of Adam's evolving cycle on his own work, noting that the process is "entirely stream of consciousness."

> He's making a form and that's generating and then it continues to generate right on over its own beginning and you go back over that hundred drawings X number of times until almost the whole field is moving but there's no "hitch," it goes and goes. So you look at it and it's so complicated that you think you're seeing a continuous animation but you realize that they're phrases that you recognize. Experienced animators looked at it and they couldn't figure it out.[29]

Ten minutes into the film, the camera moves to the center and then up, revealing the full image, a seething mass of forms, a fabulous cacophony of incredible complexity. There are the words, undulating along their path; the breasts; the unfolding lines; and globular shapes, all caught up in a rhythmic vortex around the center.

While this appears to be the apex, it is not. Unexpectedly, the color shifts, and the white center is replaced with live footage. Shapes along the edge of the center overlap the real images; he has made mattes of the moving shapes, so that he can composite the filmed images into the center. The film was shot at a high speed by Adam as he walked from his yard into the hills beyond his house, accompanied by his dog, Elvis. It was reduced in size to fit into the center, making the imagery difficult to read. Slowing down the footage, you can recognize glimpses of Elvis, Adam's shadow, and his feet, in large canvas sneakers. (Fortunately, the original film elements has been found and archived.)

The filmed journey reverses, retracing its steps, and ends; however, this still is not the end of *Dear Janice*. A copy of the fully animated drawing is composited into the center, reversed, and with the size slightly reduced. This is done again, and again, filling the entire center. Finally, the image becomes a solid gray field and displays the text "The END." The use of different musical compositions that come to an end before the next begins contributes to the disconcerting length of the film. The visual progression seems to resolve by moving into the empty center, but then the live footage appears.

Dear Janice was screened at the first presentation of CalArt's student work, in "Auditorium A213," with Kevin Thomas, a staff writer for the *Los Angeles Times*, in the audience. Thomas reports in his review of June 8, 1972:

> Unquestionably the standout film is "Dear Janice," a dazzling, dizzying animated valentine, a hopefully-to-be-shortened 16-minute swirl of colorful, fanciful, wiggly, jelly-bean shapes and fragmented messages—actually, an

> incredible 400 individual, constantly moving designs.... What Adam has done is to photograph one loop of film a dozen or so times from different distances to create a repetitive, mind-bending effect.[30]

The text of the opening credits is large and somewhat difficult to read; the loose aesthetic quality contrasts strangely with the complex and controlled animation that follows. His humor and irreverence are evident, as he wrote "Manufactured at Cal Arts," as opposed to the usual "Made at Cal Arts," and after the copyright, along with his name, is "sobeit," or "so be it" written as one word. Adam planned to revisit this film, and it may be a partial update in progress that was restored and that we now see. The opening credit includes "Infinite Animation LTD," the studio he later started, aptly named to capture the process, the evolving cycle, and his theoretical perspective.

Dear Janice was not included in the films that Adam made available through Canyon Cinema or that he sent out to festivals, undoubtedly because he considered it unfinished. The only other screening that is recorded was in November of 1972, when it was included in the Second Annual Los Angeles International Film Exposition at Grauman's Chinese Theatre, a benefit for the nonprofit organization Filmex that included a black tie "supper-reception" at the Beverly Wilshire. While there was a student film section, *Dear Janice* was included in the professional animation screening category. The first half included seven works: two from the National Film Board of Canada, four from Victor Haboush's studio, and *Dear Janice* "by a new American animator, Adam Beckett."[31]

In *Dear Janice,* images emerge and weave through space, setting the rules of the ensuing piece that, like voices in a fugue, repeat but with change and counterpoint, building a complex composition containing familiar phrases. Forms cycle, repeating, but never the same, going forward in change. Once evolved, the whole changes again, through his layering of images through the

Oxberry and the Optical Printer, truly making infinity a possibility, as he created a cosmic reality to be further explored in films yet to come.

BIBLIOGRAPHY

Beckett, Adam. California Institute of the Arts, student records for Adam K. Beckett. Courtesy Cal Arts registrar and family of Adam K. Beckett.

Engel, Jules. "Jules Engel Interview, Recalling Adam Beckett," *Adam K. Beckett: Complete Works 1970–1979*, 2011, DVD, iotaCenter.

Hofstadter, Douglas. 1979. *Godel, Escher, Bach: An Eternal Golden Braid*. New York: Basic Books.

Russett, Robert and Cecile Starr. 1976. *Experimental Animation: An Illustrated Anthology*. New York: Van Nostrand Reinhold.

Schwartz, Barry. Oral history interview with Paul Henry Brach [circa 1971]. Archives of American Art, Smithsonian Institution.

Thomas, Kevin. "Movie Reviews: 1st Cal Arts Student Films," *Los Angeles Times*, June 8, 1972.

Valley News. "44 Programs Scheduled: Winston Opens Film Expo," *Valley News* (Van Nuys, California), November 2, 1972. https://www.newspapers.com/image/30305055.

Weinstock, Nino. "Annecy '71: 8th International Cartoon Film Festival," *Graphis* 27(156), 1971–1972. Walter Herdeg, The Graphis Press, Zurich, Switzerland.

Youngblood, Gene. 1970. *Expanded Cinema*. New York: Dutton & Co. http://www.vasulka.org/Kitchen/PDF_ExpandedCinema/book.pdf.

ENDNOTES

[1] Eric Saarinen, in discussion with the author (phone), December 4, 2009.

[2] Jules Engel, "Jules Engel Interview, Recalling Adam Beckett," interviewed by Wade Ivy and Helder K. Sun, 2001, on "Adam Beckett: Complete Works 1970–1979)," 2011, iotaCenter.

[3] Paul Brach, interviewed by Barry Schwartz, "Oral History Interview with Paul Henry Brach," [circa 1971]. Archives of American Art, Smithsonian Institution. Transcript at https://www.aaa.si.edu/collections/interviews/oral-history-interview-paul-henry-brach-11865#transcript.

[4] Alison Knowles, in discussion with the author (phone), March 5, 2007.

[5] Alexander Mackendrick, letter to Adam Beckett, confirming admission, dated March 4, 1970, included in Adam's records housed at the Office of the Registrar, CalArts.

[6] Pat O'Neill, interview by the author, July 26, 2003.

[7] Barry Schrader, email to the author, April 6, 2007.

[8] Adam Beckett, Term III, 1970/1971 (March 15–June 4) CalArts student record.

[9] O'Neill, Ibid.

[10] Shalom Gorewitz, in discussion with the author (phone), February 14, 2007.

[11] Alison Knowles, in discussion with the author (phone), March 5, 2007.

[12] Michael Scroggins, in discussion with the author (phone), September 3, 2005.

[13] Gene Youngblood, *Expanded Cinema*, Dutton & Co., Inc., New York, 1970, 41. http://www.vasulka.org/Kitchen/PDF_ExpandedCinema/book.pdf.

[14] Scroggins, Ibid.

[15] Robert Russett, interview of Adam Beckett, November 1974, *Experimental Animation*, 10.

[16] Matsumi (Mike) Kanemitsu, in Adam's record for "Drawing and Draftsmanship" Term 1, 1971–1972 (November 1–January 21). CalArts student record.

[17] Pat O'Neill, in Adam's record for "Advanced Optical Printing," Term 1, 1971–1972, CalArts student record.

[18] Loring Doyle, in discussion with the author (phone), January 28, 2007.

[19] Chris Casady, in discussion with author (phone), February 5, 2003.

[20] Libby Chaney, in discussion with author (phone), January 28, 2007.

[21] Eve De Bona, email to the author, September 15, 2005.

[22] Nino Weinstock, "Annecy '71: 8th International Cartoon Film Festival," Graphis Issue No. 156, V.27, 1971–1972, 406. Walter Herdeg, Graphis Press, Zurich, Switzerland.

[23] James Gore, email to the author, November 26, 2005.

[24] David Wilson, interview by the author, March 17, 2005.

[25] Weinstock, Ibid.

[26] Dave Berry, interview by the author, February 11, 2003.

27 Douglas Hofstadter, *Godel, Escher, Bach: An Eternal Golden Braid*, New York: Basic Books, 1979, 283.

28 Youngblood, Ibid, 85.

29 O'Neill, Ibid.

30 Kevin Thomas, in "Movie Reviews: 1st Cal Arts Student Films," *Los Angeles Times*, H20, June 8, 1972.

31 "44 Programs Scheduled: Winston Opens Film Expo," (no author) *Valley News* (Van Nuys, California) November 2, 1972, 94. https://www.newspapers.com/image/30305055.

CHAPTER 5

The Evolving Artist in Eden

IN MARCH 1972, AT the end of his fifth term at CalArts, Adam was deeply immersed in creating the infinite progressions of *Dear Janice*. Three months from completing his bachelor of fine arts degree, he applied to CalArts' master of fine arts (MFA) program in Film Graphics. On his application, he wrote that he heard about the newly formed institution "From the Woodwork" and noted that his previous experience involved "a cartoon before I came here, more after I came here."[1]

His remarks under "additional information" express the hunger he had for exploring animation and the fertile ground he had found for his ideas.

> This place is the garden of eden. And so far I have managed to avoid that apple everyone says they have swallowed. After two years of work my film-making is beginning to approach critical mass. The backlog of material and ideas is beginning to give rise to a 17 minute cartoon (hopefully to be done in a few weeks). I am 5000 drawings into another one which will require much printer work to assemble.

> In addition there are 4 or 5 other ideas which must give
> rise to short films. In sum I am stuck, I can't leave this is
> the only place in the world where all this can continue to
> hopefully fruition.

Adam enrolled in two independent studies over the summer
term in order to complete his "17 minute cartoon," which was
the 16-minute *Dear Janice.* The spring term ended on March 31,
and his summer term began mid-June; however, he continued
to work and use the facilities in the interim. In his records, he
wrote that in these final independent studies, he continued his
work on "loops, cycles, and cyclic under-the camera animation,"
as well as working on a film that he referred to as "Two Yearn of
Love." That film may be what we know as *Life in the Atom,* an
animation he had begun before joining the program at CalArts.
He had also started work on "frame-by-frame sound track construction," a clue that he was broadening his attention to include
the structure and creation of sound. He was awarded his BFA
degree on August 25, 1972, and transitioned immediately into
graduate school. While his records confirm his enrollment in
the master of fine arts program, there are no course reviews. The
next nearly 3 years would be incredibly productive. CalArts provided the crucial components of free and uninterrupted time,
good equipment, and facilities.

Elsewhere, students who would emerge on the independent animation scene were improvising with what they had.
Animation had not yet been established as a dedicated course
of study within American universities in the late 1960s and
early 1970s. A noted exception is the University of California,
Los Angeles's Animation Workshop, which started in 1947.
Animation classes (not full programs) were being taught at a
number of other colleges, including the University of Southern
California, New York University, and Harvard; these would
develop into majors. John and Faith Hubley were invited to teach
animation at Harvard's new Carpenter Center for the Visual

Arts in 1963. Young people around the United States were taking film courses that might include animation techniques; however, more often, they were independently experimenting, which
invited innovation. At the University of Iowa, around 1970,
Deanna Morse used a film class assignment to deconstruct the
process of animation, intrigued by the illusion of the animated
Pillsbury Doughboy in television commercials.[2] Animator Sally
Cruikshank, whose quirky character Quasi became an independent animation icon, found herself in a similar situation at
Smith College, in Northampton, Massachusetts. She made her
first film, *Ducky*, in 1971 as an independent study project in her
senior year, with Preston Blair's animation book as her instruc-
tional resource, and using a Bolex taped to a photo enlarger.[3]
Caroline Leaf animated *Sand or Peter and the Wolf* in 1969 in
a class exploring animation taught by Derek Lamb at Radcliffe
College, which was then a sister institute of Harvard University.
Leaf was included in Russett and Starr's "Rising Generation
of Independent Animators" opening chapter of *Experimental
Animation*, along with Adam, Eliot Noyes, Jr., Laurent Coderre,
Frank Mouris, Dennis Pies (also from CalArts), John Stehura,
and Russett.

The emergence of independent animation in the United States
grew from an earnest fascination with process, image, and movement, not commercial applications. As such, Adam's work, and
that of many of his fellow independents, aligned closely with avant-
garde and experimental film, and were curated into the same
screenings at film forums, museum, university film programs,
and film festivals. As curator and historian John Hanhardt noted,
"The '70s was a crucial period for independent film distribution
and exhibition, and also there was a keen interest in animation,
independent animation."[4]

Adam aptly observed, "I think we are at the beginning of a
wonderful golden age of animation, now that the last nails are in
the coffin of the big studios."[5] In the industry, the shift of cartoons
from the movie theater to television sets had caused studios to

shut down or shrink their output. Adam, and numerous peers at CalArts, weren't interested in "cartoons," even as they developed their skills in the institute that Disney built. For those that were interested, and to be sure that cartoons were supported, a character animation area was added in 1975.

Adam was focused 100% on his films, as the institution shifted around him. At the new campus at Valencia, areas of study were separated into dedicated spaces, making it easier to be isolated from other students and changing the "family" dynamic. CalArts was near the community of Newhall, at that time a fairly rural and remote area. Many of the neighbors were suspicious of these strange art students—and faculty—who they saw as hippies and outsiders. The police constantly stopped students who had long hair. Paul Brach commented in a 1971 interview, "If the vote from this valley, the valley north of the San Fernando Valley, had been the national vote, Wallace would be president."[6]

Internally, the original, somewhat idealistic vision soon experienced growing pains, as program areas began to compete for space and funding. Alison Knowles[7] recalls an atmosphere of distrust, where the faculty suspected that people from Disney were watching the campus and were starting to question what was going on there. She, like others, could feel the winds changing and left after 3 years. Dick Higgins had already fled, as had Nam June Paik and Shuya Abe. James Tenney left in 1975. The Fluxus artists were not the only ones leaving. Woeffler left in 1973.

Despite the problems, CalArts was being noticed and attracting more students. Kathy Rose arrived from the East Coast to begin the Film Graphics graduate program in the fall of 1972. She first met Adam in the CalArts film theater, the Bijou, where all the newcomers were showing their work. "They showed my—it was really my first truly animated, drawn animated film—it was called *Movers*, which was done in drawings pads, it was all line drawing, very frenetic, very spirited with, like, dancers and percussion, but all bizarre characters with spiky hair and weird things. And I remember... he just jumped up... he got real excited."[8]

Adam was smitten by her work and by Kathy. In early 1973, they became a couple. While their individual styles were fairly different, they worked on an exquisite-corpse animation project that they called *Every Other*. Rose recalls, "He would bring over a second of animation and I would do up to a second and we would go back and forth."[9] She remembers that the drawings were shot on film, but that film was never released, and she is not sure if they ever considered it completed. A moderately damaged stack of 862 drawings survive and have been digitally recorded, with Rose's permission. *Every Other* is a playful and quirky experience, resisting a narrative, as it shows the artful and witty visual banter between the two emerging animation stars. Seeing their drawing styles juxtaposed in such a way offers a unique study, as the images are wrestled into their own style and taken down a path that the other one has to pick up and continue. There seems to be no agreed-upon goal but rather an exploration, often dissolving into sexual graphics, as per Adam's tendency.

Many friends remember this time as the happiest for Adam. Tom Barron remembers Adam's not-so-subtle courtship of Rose. Barron was recruited by Kathy, in the dorm, to help in moving a large plant that Adam had just brought for her. Barron recalls, laughing, "... he had carried about a 250-pound agave cactus that he had yanked out of the ground of one of the Valencia suburb houses, put it in his van, and dropped it in her doorway. And it was too heavy for her to move. That was his token of affection."[10]

Rose remembers Adam's personality at that time as happy and, while competitive, helpful.

> He was very tall, and he was like a Paul Bunyan kind of person. Big guy, tall.... he'd go walking down the halls, big strapping large steps and everything. But it had sort of a merry sailor quality to it. That was his vibration.[11]

In less than a year after starting the MFA program, Adam had completed two films: *Evolution of the Red Star* and *Heavy-Light*. Both screened at Los Angeles Theatre Vanguard, in "An Evening of

Abstract Films" on April 26, 1973, alongside Jules Engel's *Silence*, five films by Jordan Belson, and the computer-generated films *Poem Field No.1* by Stan VanDerBeek and Kenneth Knowlton, and *Cibernetik 5.3* by John Stehura. The evening was curated by William Moritz.

Adam, in Russett's interview, said that *Evolution of the Red Star* took 5–6 weeks to make. The date on the film credits is 1973, but it's listed on the Theatre Vanguard's program as a 1972 film. On the original drawings, Adam has signed and given a copyright date on the first and last drawings. The first drawing is dated 1974 and the last is dated 1973. (It appears that Adam would later sign his drawings and date them based on his signature, as signed drawings from *Early Animations* are dated 1975.)

Adam credits *Evolution of the Red Star* as being his "first technically successful attempt to apply my one and only original film discovery—animation of a cycle under the camera." He references Fischinger's motion painting but explains that his process, while related, involves more than one drawing or surface.

> The idea of a cycle has, needless to say, many obvious philosophical, esthetic, and scientific implications. Cycles occur in nature on all levels, from the astronomical to the psychological. The filmic idea of cyclical evolution mirrors the anti-entropic process of biological evolution. It provides an escape from static repetition by a process of positive feedback or continual addition. Aside from all of this, it is great to be able to make nice, long, fully animated films from 6 to 12 or 48 drawings.[12]

While technically efficient, as he finesses the process used in *Dear Janice*, this second film, and the first that he considers ready to put out into the world, places Adam's films firmly in what Youngblood coined as "synaesthetic cinema." They are abstract and invite more than a surface read, aspiring to engage the viewer outside of narrative language and working closer to the unconscious, inarticulate experience. The visual and sonic journey that he and composer Carl Stone created in *Evolution* invites a trance-like and experiential engagement.

Evolution of the Red Star is conceptually and structurally more mature. It is also shorter, with a running time of 7 minutes. The beginning titles employ clean, typographic fonts, not loosely painted words. It has an overarching visual structure of creation, transformation, and release that is beautifully underpinned by Stone's sound score. Adam and Stone were peers at CalArts, and had met earlier when they both attended Oakwood School, albeit in different grade levels.[13]

The "red star" of the title appears in the opening of the film as Chairman Mao's tears. Animating over an appropriated portrait, these tears emerge from the outer corner of each eye and form a continuous flow that plummets in mirrored formation and then loops back up and offscreen. Short lines radiate from his head. Chairman Mao was prominent in the news and in the psyche of America in early 1973. In March, President Nixon had become the first U.S. president to visit China. Mao's program of Communism was well known with the publication of his "Little Red Book" and was symbolically present in the red star, adorning the hat worn by Mao and his party members. Andy Warhol used a similar image of Mao to create his silk-screen print series in that same year, conferring official pop icon status on Mao.

The body of the film, after the weeping Chairman, is composed of evolving shapes and forms. A minimal, electronic tone accompanies the drawing of a red star that appears and is repeated concentrically, again and again, creating a hypnotic tunnel effect, as the star pulses and radiates. We move up to the top of the star, where a curvilinear form drawn in blue ink begins to emerge, filled with moving parallel lines that give it dimension, "like topographic maps," per Adam's description.[14] Similar forms, in red and blue, grow across the animated space. Spaces between these volumetric paths become filled with concentric squares and circles. We return to the red star and move close to see its nonuniform lines that refer to the act of drawing, putting ink on paper. The image then shifts to a void space to the left of the star, and a square appears in the now-familiar concentric movement, square within square. Here, owing to a smeared line, we can best see the incredibly short cycle that is the foundation of the complex, pulsing, and undulating space. This is the simplest demonstration of Adam's "system" of the infinite cycle, created with only six animation frames. These are not large but are on letter-sized, acme-punched paper. He begins and ends with six pieces of paper (Figure 5.1) (not including the animation of Chairman Mao), but the images at the start and finish are worlds apart.

The cycling of these drawings is not obvious to the casual eye as the camera travels into and around the surface. When the image is completed, and revealed in full, a transformation begins. Adam deftly engaged the optical printer, like a conductor with an orchestra, rephotographing the animation numerous times. The sound score is a slow, minimal call and response of singular tones and the image layers upon itself, creating variations ranging from embossed forms to flattened surfaces as the colors shift, invert, and mutate. The ever-moving lines flicker and pulse; contrast increases and then subdues; and the color changes from bold, deep purple to almost monochromatic. There is silence as the screen darkens, and then, abruptly, sound erupts in a clap of electronic thunder. The image seems electrified, strobing with intense light and color, reaching the dramatic apex of transformation. From there, the full animated frame is shown, albeit a changed, softer, brighter version, and the image and sound are resolved into a peaceful, balanced existence of "ecstatic tranquility."[15] The image of the pulsing red star returns, as the end credits appear overtop of the darkened, cycling transformation.

Stone collaborated with Adam on the piece. He was composing with a Buchla 200 audio synthesizer, working with patches and a tape recorder to do multiple passes and layering of sound. There was a kindred mindset in terms of process and generated content, as they both were creating a source and processing it in various ways. Stone remembers that the project was fun, recalling that Adam was good

FIGURE 5.1 The six animation frames used for *Evolution of the Red Star* as they appeared at the completion of drawing and animating under the camera. (Used with permission from Beckett's family.)

at communicating his ideas and had a good sense of humor, along with an occasional cranky streak. Stone would observe the emerging film with Adam to get ideas on how to proceed. He created sound to work with the images in most of the film until the final section.

... the last section has this kind of rhythmic echoing thing that happens. It's almost like a slap that echoes. And we decided to create and cut the image for that last section to the sound. So it was very dramatic because the sound was sort of following the development of the image and suddenly the relationship reversed.[16]

Adam's description of the film in his letter to Kemper at the Whitney Museum of American art (on CalArts stationery) echoes this description, noting "Some of the music was done to the completed picture and some of the animation was done to the finished music."[17]

The visual "effects" of *Evolution of the Red Star* resonate with video image processing and feedback. As established, Adam was familiar with the video synthesizer at CalArts through his participation in Paik's Critical Studies class, verified by a handcrafted certificate with Paik's name, dated December 17, 1970, that Adam kept. A typewritten description of *Evolution of the Red Star*, found in a photocopied collection of film synopses, states incorrectly that the images are video synthesized and that "VanDerBeek thought it, 'A brilliant form of optical/animation. The technical skills were considerable. Suggests the form of infinite loop.'" It also mentions that he won $60. (The source is unclear, and the text has not been found repeated in an official context.) The description, while inaccurate, illustrates that some viewers confused this work, or parts of it, with early video synthesis and image processing; it also makes apparent that synthesized video images have entered the moving image lexicon.

Adam's next film *Heavy-Light* took a further step—or rather leap—into his orchestration of images on the optical printer and, in doing so, added to the intrigue around the technology behind the images—and the image source. The picture plane is a dark void through which trails of colored light form, erupt, zigzag, swirl, and surge, congregating into swarming masses that seethe and rush toward the camera, enveloping the viewer. The film, while appearing simple in content, especially in the contemporary age of electronic color and light on a screen, is technically complex, made from an obsessive number of rephotographed layers, with time, position, scale, and color shifts on the optical printer.

The original marks that create the swarming color of *Heavy-Light* are never revealed and are transformed to such a degree that the original source, even if found, might not be recognized. One can only speculate if the source was morphing forms, as in his previous work. Colleagues and friends who remember the film connect it to live action, of a dancer or someone moving with a light source, then perhaps rotoscoped on the Oxberry. Schrader, who created the sound score, confirmed that, as with prior films, the genesis of the complex animation is from a limited source and that *Heavy-Light* was made from 13 drawings.[18] Whether these cycled or morphed is not known. Perhaps, he realized that he could create the movement of the image on the printer, as opposed to sequential drawings.

In this film, it is clear that Adam was informed by his experience in video synthesis and also the printmaking process. The drawn image is used as source material, to be layered and rephotographed, with the second pass shifted in time and, with a camera move, or move on a dial, shifted in space. Scroggins, who was in Paik's class with Adam, recalled the discussions about video as a pure art form different from film and Adam saying that he could create video feedback imagery on the optical printer.[19] Carl Stone, who worked with audio synthesis, intuited the connection, noting, "Basically what he was doing was a kind of analog feedback.... *Heavy-Light* is feedback, a feedback system. You'd take an image and process it, you'd shoot it again, changing a little bit and it's feedback. So I think that somehow, tangibly or intangibly, the work that the video guys were doing crossed over."[20]

O'Neill, who had introduced Adam to the optical printer, reflects on his process in *Heavy-Light*:

> It's curious because it looks like electronic... some kind of electronic or video signal. And it's not. But it's the same piece of animation with optical printer camera moves made.

> In other words you're into the frame and he's moving the taken part of the frame around within the boundary. And then making a master of that and then repeating many times in a print back of that, so that it has the same image repeating.[21]

The sound score that Schrader composed underpinned the imagery, echoing the ethereal yet potent movement of the colorful forms. Schrader, by then, was on the faculty at CalArts and found Adam's animations fascinating, so when Adam approached him to do the sound for *Heavy-Light,* he agreed. He was apprised of the structure of the film and given the sections to work with as they were completed. This film was going to be completely nonobjective. Schrader noted, "there's a part of me that's always appreciated abstraction, especially when it is carefully controlled and ordered, which that film is." He recalls Adam's excitement. "He was very conscious with *Heavy-Light* that he was doing... something that nobody else had done before and it was extremely original and... it was visually very powerful."[22]

Dave Berry, a friend and colleague from CalArts, is still in awe, as he recalls the film decades later:

> That's probably the peak of the optical printer. I don't think anyone's ever done what he did on an optical printer. And some of the neat stuff you can see in that film is you can see pieces of dirt wedged in between the film that got stuck in there and then multiplied thirty or forty times, you see these little boulders flying by. ... *Heavy-Light* was the one that just blew me away.[23]

Schrader recalls when the film came back from the lab with the "little boulders."

> It was a mistake but he liked it. ... it comes swirling out of the vortex and he liked that so much he left it in. He thought that was a kind of an exciting departure from the control of the rest of the stuff (Figure 5.2).[24]

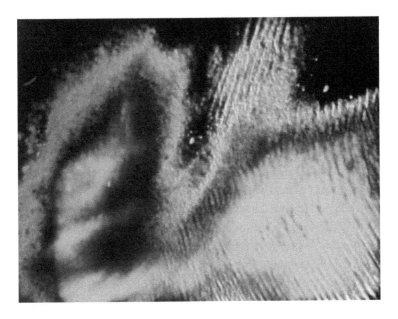

FIGURE 5.2 Still from *Heavy-Light* with dirt artifact, the small red "boulder." (Used with permission from Beckett's family.)

Evolution of the Red Star had structure, but *Heavy-Light*'s structure was tighter. Schrader recalled that it was one of the first things they discussed as they began to work together. There were three overarching sections, and each of these had three parts that elaborated on the material in different ways. This was a system, a sort of choreography that Adam devised, and, while it is not overtly obvious, the underlying order is felt in the experience of the piece. Again, he is working within an abstract vocabulary, akin to math and music. An idea, element, or "voice" is introduced and then repeated but changed, with counterpoint, a push and pull, to compose the ongoing evolution with an underlying coherency.

Adam's propensity toward math and music definitely informs the direction of his animation; we see that connection getting stronger as his work progressed. Undoubtedly, he was influenced by his first-hand knowledge of John Whitney, Sr.'s work. Perhaps, this is Adam remembering the stencils mentioned earlier and appropriating the optical printer to be his own motion control device, using the film that was being reshot as the raw material from which to create new images. Although Whitney's critical text, *Digital Harmony*, would not appear for another 7 years (1980), his discussion of dissonance, resonance, and harmony play out beautifully in Adam's film and attest to the potency of his early interactions with Whitney.

Heavy-Light is Adam's dialog with video technology and with the ephemeral, and transcendental, presence of light. His composed aurora borealis of cascading light resonates with Thomas Wilfred's mysterious Lumia art compositions that are "played" on the machines that he innovated, some compositions not repeating for months. While Adam may not have seen Wilfred's work firsthand, he undoubtedly knew of it. A quote from Thomas Wilfred opens the "Intermedia" chapter of *Expanded Cinema* and aptly captures Adam's motivation to "express the human longing which light has always symbolized, a longing for greater reality, a cosmic consciousness, a balance between the human entity and the great common denominator, the universal rhythmic flow."[25] Wilfred's work was actively exhibited; his "Lumia Suite, Opus 158" was installed in the Museum of Modern Art (MoMA) from 1964 to 1980, and there was a retrospective of his work there in 1971.

Jordan Belson's *Light* and Stan Brakhage's *The Text of Light* appeared in 1973 and 1974, respectively. Youngblood's evocative description of Belson's work could just as easily be referring to Adam's *Heavy-Light*. "In their amorphous, gaseous, cloudlike imagery it is colour, not line, which defines the forms that ebb and flow across the frame with uncanny impact. It is this stunning emotional force that lifts the films far beyond any realm of 'purity' into the most evocative and metaphysical dimensions of sight and sound."[26] Brakhage's *The Text of Light* also uses nonobjective forms of light but differs, as it stays grounded in the film experience, as the viewer watches the phenomena of refracted light in front of a static (although shaky at times) camera.

Adam's intention can be inferred from experiencing his work projected large on a screen. Clues can be gleaned from the synopses he provided for catalogs and screenings, from the Russett interview and from studying the numerous sketchbooks and ephemera that he left behind. It was through art and animation that he explored and perhaps tried to make sense of his conscious and unconscious self. In his descriptions for *Flesh Flows,* he speaks of a "spirit of contemplation" and a "feeling of tranquility" is noted in his verbiage for *Evolution of the Red Star.* (That would be at the end, well after the loud clap that never fails to startle the audience!)

In the trajectory of Adam's released films, *Heavy-Light* is undoubtedly the zenith of his innovation and a significant step toward his quest for transcendental experience in film. However, it wasn't as successful as his other films, perhaps due to the concurrent appearance of the "light" films by the more established artists. It didn't appear in the 1976 American Federation of the Arts catalog, and his description of *Heavy-Light* that appeared in the Canyon Cinema catalog downplays the film. The excitement that Adam had expressed, and that Schrader remembers as they were working on the film, is not reflected here.

> This is one of those abstract animated films in which colored, richly textured light moves in a black, three-dimensional space. The pictures and the electronic score are unified in a strict structure made of three main sections, which progressively develop three subsections. This film may look like it was made using computers or video to the uninitiated, but only animation and mucho optical printing are to be seen herein.[27]

O'Neill believes that the film, while successful, in some ways didn't have the appeal of his previous work. "The problem was when the film was finished it was so perfectly executed that it looked like something that would be very easy to do with video. And it lost the spontaneity that the drawing had." He explains that Adam had an idea, a process that he was pursuing, and there was no way to really be sure how it would turn out.

> I don't think he even realized that it was going to wind up... looking electronic. He was into the process and everybody sort of said, oh this will be interesting. And it *was* but it was sort of... it kind of became... cold. And I don't think he pursued that direction any further after that.[28]

Video and electronic music offered real-time results. Adam was working abstractly, following a vision in his head, a plan on paper, working for hours, or days, in the studio. While he had an amazing mathematical ability and obsessive concentration, things didn't always go as planned. O'Neill remembers Adam working on the optical printer as he was creating *Heavy-Light*.

> He didn't know what it was going to turn into. He just worked and worked and worked on this thing. It was very labor intensive because every frame you're making an exact move on the dials. I remember when he was working on that he'd be in there for... a day and a half, with the whole thing in his head. And then he would screw up and he'd just explode and there'd be screaming and there'd be the sound of someone rushing against the walls in the printer room. ... So then he'd storm out of there and then he'd come back later and do it all again.[29]

After shooting, he'd have to wait for his film to return from the lab to see the results of his experiments. Stone remembers asking Adam about how it was to work without seeing or hearing the results immediately and that he responded that it was like Christmas, getting film back from the lab. This process, Stone confirmed, was truly exciting for Adam; he really wasn't sure about what he would get back.[30]

Stone, while working in electronic music, credits Adam's processes as an influence, noting the layering and sequencing, so that one loses sense of the original material. "All of the small details drop away and you're left with a kind of meta-image."

The late Richard "Dr." Baily was at CalArts from 1975 to 1977 and also points to the impact Adam's approach to imagery made on his own work.

> ... these tools were instruments just like musical instruments and they could be looked at in different ways, not just photographing a piece of film, they really were like musical instruments.... So that's the idea, that Adam could make this movie like *Heavy Light* out of nothing, to pull it out of thin air. ... Yeah, you could deal with the equipment on its own level. Instead of forcing it to speak English you could speak to it in its own language.[31]

Baily developed his own animation system, "Spore," to create art as well as commercial work through his company Image Savant. He noted a kinship between his system and Adam's process. For the 2000 movie *The Cell*, Baily created a sequence strongly inspired by Adam's *Heavy-Light* and declared that the results were "just pure Beckett"! The sequence, about two-thirds of the way through the movie, is an abstract visualization of the transition from the lab into the mind of a serial killer. In a both sly and gracious gesture, Baily acknowledged Adam's influence by having an honorary credit for Adam, as technical advisor with Image Savant, appear in the film's credits.

Another tangible marker of influence comes from Robert Luttrell, who had been making films in Amsterdam in 1973 and traveled to London to attend a film festival. It was there that Luttrell saw *Heavy-Light* and the work of Pat O'Neill. He also learned about CalArts. He says, "I decided to go *back* specifically because I saw his film. And then when I was changing the name of my corporation I named it after the film that I saw then—*Heavy-Light*."[32]

Adam's peers were also influenced by his intense drive and motivation to create his films, complete them with titles and credits, and then work just as hard to get them out to the viewing public. Rose affirms this, stating:

> I'm sure he had a really strong influence because for one thing... he really completed things that were major, real works. ... it was the kind of place where that sort of thing happened and he was one of the people who added to that energy.[33]

The obsessive work in the studio was continued through the process of printing and distribution. Tom Barron recalls:

> He was also crazy like a fox, because he made a really strict rule out of getting his films printed properly, put them in fiber boxes and sent them out to every film festival known to man. ... He totally got that. And consequently he was seen in a lot of different festivals and well known in the film community.[34]

Evolution of the Red Star and *Heavy-Light* were printed and submitted to numerous festivals and began their public life. They were both included in the 1973 Sinking Creek Film Festival and in the 1974 Humboldt Film Festival, and others. Adam's reputation as a star on campus was established. With these two films, he began to make ripples in the broader animation community.

BIBLIOGRAPHY

Beckett, Adam. California Institute of the Arts, student records for Adam K. Beckett. Courtesy CalArts registrar and family of Adam K. Beckett.

Beckett, Adam. *Letter to Terry Kemper.* New York: Frances Mulhall Achilles Library, Archives, Whitney Museum of American Art, NY. John Hanhardt artist files, Box 3, Adam Beckett folder.

Canyon Cinema Cooperative Catalog #4, 1976. Canyon Cinema, San Francisco, CA: Warren's Waller Press.

New American Filmmakers: Selections from the Whitney Museum of American Art Film Program, 1976. New York: American Federation of the Arts.

Russett, Robert and Cecile Starr. 1976. *Experimental Animation: An Illustrated Anthology*. New York: Van Nostrand Reinhold.

ENDNOTES

1. Adam Beckett, California Institute of the Arts, Admissions Application, MFA, dated March 31, 1972.
2. Deanna Morse, email to the author, April 6, 2014.
3. Sally Cruikshank, Wikipedia entry, https://en.wikipedia.org/wiki/Sally_Cruikshank, and "Sally Cruikshank: A Career Retrospective, Part 1." http://www.artofthetitle.com/feature/sally-cruikshank-a-career-retrospective-part-one/.
4. John Hanhardt, discussion with the author (phone), July 19, 2005.
5. Russett, interview of Adam Beckett, November 1974, *Experimental Animation*, 11.
6. Paul Brach, interviewed by Barry Schwartz, "Oral History Interview with Paul Henry Brach," [circa 1971]. Archives of American Art, Smithsonian Institution. https://www.aaa.si.edu/collections/interviews/oral-history-interview-paul-henry-brach-11865#transcript.
7. Alison Knowles, in discussion with the author (phone), March 5, 2007.
8. Kathy Rose, interview by the author, March 18, 2004.
9. Ibid.
10. Tom Barron, in discussion with the author (phone), August 24, 2004.
11. Rose, Ibid.
12. Russett, Ibid., 11.
13. Carl Stone, interview by the author, March 5, 2003.
14. Beckett's synopsis for *Evolution of the Red Star*, "New American Filmmakers: Selections from the Whitney Museum of American Art Film Program" 1976 catalog, American Federation of the Arts, 75.
15. Beckett's synopsis for *Evolution of the Red Star, Canyon Cinema Cooperative Catalog #4*. 1976 Canyon Cinema, Inc., San Francisco, CA: Warren's Waller Press, 17.
16. Stone, Ibid.

17 Beckett's, letter to Terry Kemper, dated August 6, 1974. Frances Mulhall Achilles Library, Archives, Whitney Museum of American Art, NY. John Hanhardt artist files, Box 3, Adam Beckett folder.

18 Barry Schrader, interview by the author, October 1, 2004.

19 Michael Scroggins, in discussion with the author (phone), September 3, 2005.

20 Stone, Ibid.

21 O'Neill, interview by the author, July 26, 2003.

22 Schrader, Ibid.

23 Dave Berry, interview by the author, February 11, 2003.

24 Schrader, Ibid.

25 Thomas Wilfred, quoted in Youngblood's *Expanded Cinema*, 345. (No source for quote. May have been from interview. Wilfred died in 1968.)

26 Youngblood, 157–158.

27 Beckett's synopsis for *Heavy-Light, Canyon Cinema Cooperative Catalog #4*. 1976 Canyon Cinema, Inc., San Francisco, CA: Warren's Waller Press, 17.

28 O'Neill, Ibid.

29 Ibid.

30 Stone, Ibid.

31 Richard "Dr." Baily, discussion with the author (phone), July 11, 2004.

32 Rob Luttrell, discussion with the author (phone), June 13, 2006.

33 Rose, Ibid.

34 Barron, Ibid.

CHAPTER 6

From the Carnal to the Cosmic

*E*VOLUTION OF THE RED *Star* and *Heavy-Light* secured Adam's reputation as a rising star and set the pace for a busy 1974. He released two new films early in the year: *Flesh Flows* and *Sausage City*. Adam was spending many hours scouting out opportunities to show his work, completing and submitting entry forms, shipping canisters of film, and animating. In 1972, he had written on his application that he found himself in Eden and had what he needed. Two years later, he applied for a leave of absence from school, giving the reason that he needed more time to finish his thesis animation. He indicated his intention to be away for one session and return in the fall of 1974 or perhaps even earlier, in the summer session. Officially no longer a student, he was still very much a presence on campus, using the equipment and his Valencia post office box as the address for shipping and receiving his films.

His request to postpone his degree was dated March 25, 1974, the same date of an invoice for the rental of three of his films, at $10 each. The invoice, and a letter dated March 26, is an early correspondence with Ron Epple of Picture Start, an independent film distribution company in Champaign, Illinois.[1] Adam thanks Epple for his interest in the films and informs him that prints of *Evolution of the Red Star, Sausage City*, and *Flesh Flows* were on the way and that his "print situation" is tight, as the Ann Arbor festival is keeping his films to include in their touring show that year.

Adam launched his production studio, Infinite Animation Ltd., that same year.[2] This name cleverly expressed his obsessive approach to animation, specifically his use of the evolving cycle that could repeat ad infinitum, even as it mutated under the hand of the artist. It first appears in the opening credits of *Sausage City*. (The restored version of *Dear Janice* has the studio name in the credits, as noted earlier.)

He engaged in the local animation and film community, attending screenings and participating. He created the animated opening title for the 9th International Tournée of Animation; earlier, he had created an extravagant cycle as an intermission for the 7th Tournée, with a rubber-stamped cycle of "More to Come" moving in multiples, filling the screen. The Tournée, created by ASIFA-Hollywood, with Prescott Wright heading the programming, was an important outlet for American animation, while at the same time bringing animation from around the world to audiences in the United States. In addition to the opening sequence, Adam's *Flesh Flows* was included with 12 other selections in the 9th Tournée program. His work was in the company of films from Italy, Belgium, Canada, and Yugoslavia, projected on the screen at the Los Angeles County Museum of Art's Bing Theater on April 12, 1974.[3] The opening sequence is quintessential Adam, with text on a background of flowing color emerging from a fixed, drawn source, similar to *Flesh Flows* but with many more repetitions, so that the source of the image is at no time discernible.

By the fall of 1974, Adam was clearly established as a force in independent animation in America. He received an American Film Institute (AFI) grant for a new film, *Knotte Grosse*, in October, for the significant amount (especially in 1974) of \$9,275.[4] In November, *Flesh Flows* won the bronze Hugo award for student film at the Chicago International Film Festival; Kathy Rose's *Mirror People* won the gold. John Hanhardt selected three of Adam's animations for inclusion in the program titled simply "Animation," appearing in late November as part of the New American Filmmakers series at the Whitney Museum of American Art. There, Adam's *Flesh Flows, Sausage City,* and *Evolution of the Red Star* played alongside the work of his mentor, Jules Engel, as well as that of Robert Russett, Lillian Schwartz and Ken Knowlton, Steve Segal, Alan Slasor, and Lorraine Bubar. Only Adam had more than two films included in the show.

Russet interviewed Adam in November of 1974, perhaps as a result of seeing Adam's work in the Whitney program. As seen in previous chapters, this interview provided two pages of invaluable communication from Adam about his work, influences, and experience up to that point and provided one of the few records of Adam's perspective and intention. When asked about his films, Adam stated that he had finished four films and had "two in the works," *Life in the Atom* and a new version of *Dear Janice,* which would suggest that one of these was intended as the MFA animation, for which he needed more time to make. It is striking that he did not mention *Knotte Grosse,* especially as he had recently received the AFI award to support making it. Adam referred to his work in "special effects," which he planned to pursue, citing the opening title that he created for the 9th International Tournée of Animation as an example. It is a prescient note for what was to come. When asked what attracted him to animation, he replied, "It moves; it can be a one-man show or even a spectacle." As to his interest in narrative that is not verbal, Adam responded that his "main interest is still in the visual image itself" and that he is "interested in the problems of creating coherent and organic visual compositions in time."[5]

Flesh Flows demonstrates Adam's maturing skill at creating these "organic visual compositions" in this experiential journey that is both sensual and transformative. It is his most person-ally ambitious work, connecting his interests in the erotic to his pursuit of the spiritual in a film that moves from the "carnal to the cosmic," as he wrote in his Canyon Cinema catalog synopsis. Youngblood's *Expanded Cinema*, again, provides a critical con-text for Adam's work in considering "synaesthetic cinema," a cin-ema that has evolved beyond montage and order. The content is the filmmaker's awareness; new cinema is where "man attempts to express a total phenomenon—his own consciousness."[6] This idea resonates throughout Adam's films as well as his numerous draw-ings. His animations are able to unfurl through time and implied space, with the unimaginable visuals made possible through his technical agility on the optical printer. As Youngblood wrote perceptively, the ability to "explore new dimensions of aware-ness requires new technological extensions."[7] While Youngblood was considering the potential of new technologies to expand our consciousness, in the vein of McLuhan, Adam was pursuing new extensions of *existing* technology, redefined through his innova-tive approach.

Throughout Adam's sketchbooks and drawings, we find the human form, from realistic to abstract, suggesting the subject's psychedelic experiences while offering insight into the psyche of the artist (Figure 6.1). Bodies often appear to be melting, trans-forming, or dissolving into geometric bits. Depictions of sexual intercourse appear, often with exaggerated proportions; large phallic forms appear almost as another limb in a tangle of limbs. These, not unlike the erotic forms that appear at the start of the film, speak to the physical, as well as psychological, experience of sex, somewhat surreal and sometimes humorous. There are erotic drawings that are also rather grotesque, with human and animal

FIGURE 6.1   Life drawing showing motion and dissolving persona, in active, detailed style. (Used with permission from Beckett's family.)

forms melding, and orgies, such as the bizarre onstage scene with the title "The Ed Sylvan Show," dated 1969 (Figure 6.2).

Youngblood addressed films that depicted sexual relations and explored sex as a part of the varied human experience, citing Carolee Schneemann's *Fuses* (1967) and Paul Morrissey's *Flesh* (1968). Coining the phrase "polymorphous eroticism," he writes that expanded cinema has the ability to "liberate man from centuries of sexual ignorance so that he may at last understand the infinite sensorium that is himself."[8] Adam's *Flesh Flows* depicts the genital being, the physically ideated self, liberating it through metamorphoses into pulsing light and color.

FIGURE 6.2 Imaginative on-stage orgy, titled the "The Ed Sylvan Show," dated 1969. (Used with permission from Beckett's family.)

Adam, in his description of the film, explained that it is structured as three "chapters."[9] The first chapter is of hand-drawn, metamorphosing, surreal, and erotic forms; the second chapter repeats the first but soon adds layers that phase in time and space, via optical printing; and the third, final chapter repeats again but goes further and deeper, taking the images, and the viewer, to the apex of transformation. Here, we see a more deliberate, mature artist, adept at pacing, timing, and structure, able to show restraint and also take command of the sound. The sound score is understated, each iteration building gradually to reach the ultimate transformation. (The sound design is discussed further in the following chapter.)

Adam abandoned the typographic font used in the titles of his previous two films, returning to drawn text. The morphing shapes of his opening credits demonstrate, through their fluid, weighted movement, the animation skill that he has now mastered. The body of the animation, as it were, begins with phallic characters engaged in the genital experience of sex. At the start, there appears to be two "couples," with one member being the orifice and the other the probe; one couple merges, still interacting but as a single unit. One character is a penis with legs. No entity has eyes or arms. These disembodied genital beings probe and lick until the scene erupts into organic—or orgasmic—shapes that fill the space, resolving into a complex, abstract labyrinth. This reorganizes into mountains of breasts surrounding a valley; at its end, a floating pair of breasts evolves into a female form, albeit one without a head, arms, or legs. She distorts into ribbons of entangled, geometric abstractions, reforming into the female torso, now with three breasts. (This may sound familiar.) A rabbit emerges from the pouch belly of the truncated woman, and the rabbit's arms and ears become part of the maze-like structure that dominates the space. A contrasting egg shape emerges and cracks, and the beak of a large toucan-like bird appears, but as soon as its head becomes discernible, the forms dissipate and reform into a hand, with the palm facing outward.

When considering his conceptual and artistic use of morphosis, *Flesh Flows* is the most definitive work for Adam. The animated narrative, from the probing penises and tongues to the hand at the end, is a study of morphs, from objective to nonobjective, employing morphing transitions to move the "story" from scene to scene. While the changing forms of *Dear Janice*, and later, *Sausage City*, never transcend their cycling evolutions, caught in a loop, the morphing forms that are the foundation of *Flesh Flows* finally transcend into another state, via Adam's alchemic genius on the optical printer. The entire metamorphosing sequence becomes a cycle, with the second and third "chapters" changed through multiple passes of rephotography. He is morphing the image that is in the flow of change already, freeing it from its grounding in the recognizable to the final absolute transmogrified glow of color and form and ultimately to the void of the white screen.

Adam downplays the complexity of the film with his characteristic playful language in a letter to Terry Kemper, who was coordinator of the film program at the Whitney Museum. "This film has some of the first animation I ever did included in the flow. That old standby of beginning animators, namely transformation, is given its just desserts by being transformed in turn on the optical printer."[10] *Flesh Flows* is based on drawings that he started 5 years earlier, either at Antioch or on his own. Many of the drawings debuted in *Early Animations or Quacked Jokes*; segments are edited and reshot to create the foundation for *Flesh Flows*. In the 1974 incarnation, the timing of the movement is smoother, and the image is also flipped and framed differently. The headless, armless nude female that emerges from the title text "Quacked Jokes" appears in *Flesh Flows*, smaller in the picture plane, created from the female form that appears at the end of the valley surrounded by breasts. Adam has repurposed these sequences, eliminating sections as they appeared in the earlier work, creating a cohesive new whole with morphing transitions. The opening section of probing genital beings in *Flesh Flows* doesn't appear in the earlier film, but these drawings were created prior to his arrival at CalArts, as evidenced by the drawings (Figure 6.3). They

FIGURE 6.3   Probing genital beings in *Flesh Flows,* vertically oriented on paper with nail-punched holes. (Used with permission from Beckett's family.)

are all vertically oriented on paper with nail-punched holes for registration. His reuse of the images demonstrates a consistent and continued interest in sexual experience as the subject matter, here reimagined with nearly 5 years of animation and optical printing experience.

The physical experience of sex, in the first "chapter," is more metaphysical than physical, with the possible exception of the erotic characters of the opening sequence. The female form, without face or identity, has the symbolic presence similar to prehistoric carved objects that were the agent of fertility—as are the egg and the rabbit—and change. The created experience is surreal, inhabiting the mental space of the mind rather than the body. The ensuing transformations on the optical printer push the transcendental state further, as the images themselves change from abstractions to the hallucinogenic surreal. The drawn forms become less discernible in the sea of feathery lines that phase through the space of the picture plane. A body, then a hand, is recognized briefly before being swallowed up in the luminous seething mass. The only drawings that are not completely altered are the genital beings at the start of each chapter; these flip in orientation, but their beginning motions remain unaltered by optical printing.

With the final iteration, matter has become energy, and we are a part of it, pulled through the zooming motion into the space of the image. After the brief glimpse at the opening erotic forms, all recognizable forms disappear, except for a liminal moment, when the torso of the female coalesces in the center of the frame, lines radiating around her. She disappears, and the transformation into nonobjective imagery accelerates. The density of repeated lines creates near-solid shapes of color. Having achieved a state of complete transmutation, everything dissipates into a white void.

Adam was known for doing everything to the "nth degree,"[11] as his friend and colleague Dave Berry fondly recalled, and we see that trait brilliantly illustrated in this film. He is revisiting a technique that he perfected, perhaps too well, in *Heavy-Light*. With this newer film, he allows us to see the drawings that are the erotic origin of the fantastic spectacle of color and light, giving us a human point of reference, grounding us in the experience.

Flesh Flows is connected to Adam's unfinished *Life in the Atom*, a film that explored the theme of a sexual relationship more explicitly. (Berry recalls that *Flesh Flows* was created from the outtakes of that film.) As noted earlier, Adam began *Life in the Atom* as early as 1968, continuing to work on it over the years but never completing it. Accordingly, the version that was restored reads as a disjointed piece, having been assembled—and disassembled— over time. In the Russett interview, Adam describes it simply as "some rather ornate animation of an attractive young couple and their activities."[12] It is a visual narrative that expresses the *sensation* of love and sexual relationship of a couple, a simple and perhaps idealistic premise for an 18 year old. The progressive explicitness of the images and the more embodied animated movement reflect the evolving culture as well as the experience of an artist moving from late adolescence to adulthood.

Life in the Atom's somewhat disjointed collection of segments provides an invaluable touchstone for Adam's progress and development, both personally and artistically. The style and skill fluctuate throughout the piece, coinciding with when they were drawn and animated. Some of the drawings were nail-punched and vertically oriented, predating his arrival at CalArts, where he transitioned to the norm of horizontal, Acme hole-punched paper. Earlier segments have a simpler drawing style, and the animation lacks weight and pacing. This is seen at the start of the film, where an ambiguous nude couple has slow, weightless movement as they embrace and interact. They do not engage in sex. Later additions evidence deft attention to detail and controlled movement. The movement and drawings of the final scene, for instance, are much more refined and more explicit, moving from sensual and erotic to what could arguably be described as pornographic. The couple is blatantly copulating, with an emphasis on the immense, thrusting phallus; aroused vulva; and massive testicles, whose swinging motion more than adequately demonstrates the animation principles of follow-through and overlapping motion.

The artist, and the man, has clearly progressed in his experience of both animation and sex.

The title of the film, while never explicitly stated, is a play on "Adam" and "atom," alluding to life in the mind, the universe, of Adam. The film opens with live footage of him stationed at the Oxberry animation stand. We are looking down, from his perspective; the image on the stand is a horizon line that fluctuates slightly as two drawings alternate. His left hand is moving back and forth along the bottom of the shooting area, and a pad of exposure sheets with notes lays on his left. The camera moves into the image on the stand, and a black matte dissolves in, replacing Adam and his environment and framing the ensuing animated world.

The couple that opens the film reflects an ideal; they are nondescript, placeholders for male and female. They speak via word balloons that contain unreadable words, as do some of the characters in his comics. A fish-like creature appears screen left, in the air next to the couple; it also has a word balloon, but instead of scribbles, it contains music notes. The scene is more surreal than sensual; this heightens as the woman's arms stretch and curve, and a dog clambers over the hill, running past them. They all morph, stretching and melding into a labyrinth of organic form, similar to that seen in *Flesh Flows*. The timing of the animation does not vary, devoid of weight or gesture, an evidence of early, still-developing animation skills.

There is a mix of surrealism and abstraction as the scenes flow from one segment to another. A squat man with frog-like features emerges, fairly imaginative and detailed. His feet are of different sizes and oriented differently to the body. His hands also have a strange relationship to the body, which is a characteristic observed in a number of Adam's characters. The hands do not seem to be on the correct arm, and the palm and thumb are oddly drawn. Yet, in his stacks of life drawings, beautifully executed drawings of hands and feet are found, attesting to his skill (Figure 6.4). His animated characters have strange appendages, being drawn as straight-ahead animation in the process of

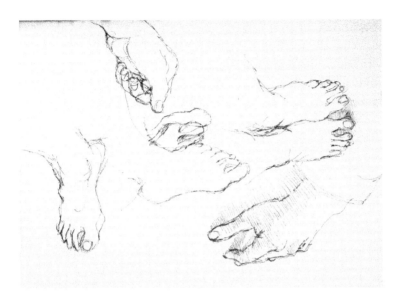

FIGURE 6.4   Adam was a skilled draftsman, capable of rendering realistic hands and feet. (Used with permission from Beckett's family.)

morphing. Odd hands appear in a number of Adam's drawings and on the mysterious man in *Sausage City.*

As the character transforms, he pulls a cube from under his hat. The cube unfolds, providing the setting for a statue-like woman, without arms or legs, and a man. They evolve into an erotic couple, with the man's penis growing inordinately large. Their limbs elongate into ribbon-like shapes, their bodies disappear into abstraction, but their genitals remain recognizable—and active. The red, black, and white colors of the scene become more pronounced until the forms finally erupt in abstracted blobs, with her breasts being the last recognizable shape. Perhaps, as in *Flesh Flows*, this depicts transcending the carnal; however, it reads more readily as the abstracted experience of orgasm.

The climatic blobs, drawn in color pencil, are reminiscent of the organic forms in *Dear Janice*. Here, however, they quickly change into a more purposefully, cleanly drawn evolving cycle of rounded, organic shapes. Some are black, with white lines bisecting the form into parts (Figure 6.5). The cycle continues with the origin point hidden deftly. The pattern is mesmerizing, order within chaos. The color inverts to white lines on a black background, creating a matte as he builds numerous layers via

FIGURE 6.5 Unused drawing of black organic shapes, with a comic addition commenting on a mistake; from the *Life in the Atom*. (Used with permission from Beckett's family.)

the optical printer. From here, he reverses back to the original shapes, providing a good place to devise a transition to his next segment. These links are integral to his protracted progress, enabling him to weave together the newly drawn sequences with the older ones.

The organic shapes diversify, and the framing of the shot changes to reveal that the genesis of these morphing forms is a deftly drawn vagina. Its owner wears a ribbon tied in a bow on her head, confounding innocence and sexual corporeality. She is wearing Mary Janes, traditionally children's shoes, while stroking her ample breasts. She grabs two small blobs to create a skirt, and a top appears that allows her breasts to remain visible.

Again, noncontemporaneous sections are bridged with the morphing of forms that then reform into the next segment. Here, a door opens and a hand places a small rocket on a ledge. It launches itself, and the symbolism is not to be missed, as the geometric mass that produced the rocket becomes a male, sitting cross-legged, with Mickey Mouse ears and a large, erect phallus that he strokes with both hands. This scene then transforms into the couple that we recognize from the opening sequence. We have returned full circle; however, their story is not over. The dog turns to look at them and then runs and jumps into the open mouth of a sharp-toothed head that appears over the horizon. The man, with one arm around the woman, takes the floating head in his hand, and it disappears momentarily, reforming as a ball that rises up to become a smiling sun. It is smiling at the couple; the man's penis has grown enormous, and the couple is entangling in erotic glee.

While the earlier scenes are sexual, the ending segment skirts the boundary of pornography owing to the explicit nature of the animated genitalia, as noted earlier. His visage throughout this final scene is not stable. A helmet appears and then transforms to reference a Mickey Mouse hat. Are these Adam's varied, unstable alter egos, or does this indicate the intrusion of a new lover? The

woman, while evolving, appears to be the same person throughout and resembles his drawings of fellow animator Kathy Rose,
who was his girlfriend from 1972 through 1974. The exception is
the persona with the hair ribbon wearing Mary Janes.

The female, when present, is the foregrounded character. We see
her as the womb source, as the companion in the opening scene,
receiving—and eating—a flower from her mate and as the object
of desire in the red, black, and white segment. In the end, she is
the receiver, a stabilized character that is the source of pleasure
for a changing, unstable, and dominant male character. Based on
the drawing, the animation skill, and the shift from the symbolic
to the more experiential, this final segment appears to have been
created after or around the end of his relationship with Rose.

Two stacks of drawings that relate directly to *Life in the Atom*
were found and may have been included, or intended for inclusion,
in a different version of this planned magnum opus. Each sequence
has a couple that is constantly morphing and mostly nude but not
nearly as explicit as the final couple in *Life in the Atom*. In one,
the woman emerges from a duck-like cartoon figure and then
morphs into a buxom mouse human (à la Minnie Mouse). In both,
the man is an unstable character, often taking grotesque form
(Figure 6.6). The drawings, especially those of the mouse woman,
are refined. They are on large, animation paper (12½" by 10½").
The two sequences connect, even though they are numbered as
a distinct series of drawings, with one going from 1 to 415 and
the second series (that had *Bouncés Ball* on a title sheet) numbered
267–520. The beginning of *Bouncés Ball* has turned brown, visible
in the posthumously animated version included on the DVD. The
numerous images that make up *Early Animations, Flesh Flows,
Life in the Atom,* and these 668 drawings clearly demonstrate that
the morphing, sexually engaged couple emerging into and out of
abstraction was a significant preoccupation for Adam.

It is helpful to remember that he began this film at or near the
age of 18 years and worked on it through his twenties. During
this time, he had few known girlfriends other than Rose. John

FIGURE 6.6 Animation frame from the sequence titled *Bouncés Ball*. (Used with permission from Beckett's family.)

Koenig, his friend from childhood onward, noted that Adam had "passions" that often didn't go anywhere, as he wouldn't follow through, being awkward, or the women did not reciprocate.[13] He revered women, as evident in several comics of him and Rose and in his drawings and doodles (Figure 6.7). One exemplary board filled with text and images reflects love for Libby Chaney, whom he had met through Koenig's mother, the artist Cathy Heerman. Chaney spent time with Adam and considered him a friend.[14] The art board offers insight into his thinking and his questions and prominently displays Chaney's name several times, attesting to his feelings that surpassed friendship. Christine Bleakley may have been his last acknowledged girlfriend; they met at an Industrial Light and Magic (ILM) party and were a couple for a few months, remaining friends afterward.[15]

FIGURE 6.7   Comic by Adam showing his devotion to and depiction of Rose. (Used with permission from Beckett's family.)

Numerous friends and colleagues recall seeing *Life in the Atom* in its incomplete form and thinking that it was remarkable and groundbreaking. His teacher and mentor, Jules Engel, was purportedly disturbed by the work, considering it pornographic, which it would have been by the standards of Engels' generation and cultural background. If *Life in the Atom* was planned as Adam's thesis, Engel's disapproval may have been the reason why Adam interrupted his graduate studies.

When Adam began working on it, in the late 1960s, the naked body and the act of sex were not just accepted; these were rampant, appearing in underground comix and in Bakshi's popular animated movies *Fritz the Cat* (1972) and *Heavy Traffic* (1973). Similar imagery is seen in the more obscure independent animation *Black Pudding* (1969) by British animation artist Nancy Edell.[16] The naked human body was used to create satire and cause discomfort to those who veered toward more conservative norms. As a teenager, Adam had lived with drawings by John Altoon, whose work from the 1960s included drawings of the human body that tended toward the grotesque, with marks and gestures suggesting frayed sensibilities and engagement. This raw approach was native to Adam's experience and his work.

However, culture was changing, as people faced the harsh reality of the time, including the energy crisis, Watergate, and the lingering psychological aftermath of the murders by Charles Manson and his followers. The 1960s were long gone, replaced by a strange, uneasy conservatism. America was "growing up," but Adam may not have negotiated that change easily, having been steeped in the freedom of the Hog Farm and a childhood of art and comfort. Adam knew that times were changing and that *Life in the Atom* would not be received as it was intended. Berry confirmed this: "I remember him saying that he thought that culture was going to go another way and that it had turned in the wrong direction which made this film anachronistic."[17] Adam had spent years working on a film that he would not be able to screen publicly.

For years, *Life in the Atom* was a mystery, not found in the many film elements collected from family, friends, and print labs. After years of searching, a print was found by Beth Block, a filmmaker who had known Adam and had lived near him. This was added to the numerous film elements and prints at the Academy Film Archive and slated for restoration work. Appropriately, a sound score was created by Carl Stone to accompany the restored version, 37 years after their collaboration on *Evolution of the Red Star*.

BIBLIOGRAPHY

American Federation of the Arts. 1976. *New American Filmmakers: Selections from the Whitney Museum of American Art Film Program*. New York: American Federation of the Arts.

Beckett, Adam. 1976. *Canyon Cinema Cooperative Catalog #4*. Canyon Cinema, San Francisco, CA: Warren's Waller Press.

Champlin, Charles. "Critic at Large: The Moving Art of Animation," *Los Angeles Times*, April 12, 1974. ProQuest Historical Newspapers, *Los Angeles Times*.

Russett, Robert and Cecile Starr. 1976. *Experimental Animation: An Illustrated Anthology*. New York: Van Nostrand Reinhold.
Youngblood, Gene. 1970. *Expanded Cinema*. New York: Dutton & Co. http://www.vasulka.org/Kitchen/PDF_ExpandedCinema/book.pdf.

ENDNOTES

1. Adam Beckett letter to Ron Epple, March 25, 1975. Private papers, courtesy of Deirdre Beckett.
2. Robert Russett, interview of Adam Beckett, November 1974, *Experimental Animation*, 10.
3. Champlin, Charles, "Critic at Large: The Moving Art of Animation," *Los Angeles Times*, April 12, 1974, p. OC_C1. ProQuest Historical Newspapers, *Los Angeles Times*.
4. B. Caroline Sisneros (Librarian, Louis B. Mayer Library, American Film Institute) email message to the author, July 22, 2004.
5. Russett, 11.
6. Gene Youngblood, *Expanded Cinema*, Dutton & Co., Inc., New York, 1970. http://www.vasulka.org/Kitchen/PDF_ExpandedCinema/book.pdf, 76.
7. Youngblood, 136.
8. Youngblood, 116–117.
9. Adam Beckett's description in the "New American Filmmakers: Selections from the Whitney Museum of American Art Film Program" 1976 catalog, 75. American Federation of the Arts.
10. Adam Beckett, letter to Terry Kemper, dated August 6, 1974. Frances Mulhall Achilles Library, Archives, Whitney Museum of American Art, NY. John Hanhardt artist files, Box 3, Adam Beckett folder.
11. Dave Berry, interview by the author, February 11, 2003.
12. Russett, 11.
13. John Koenig, in discussion with the author (phone), June 21, 2006.
14. Libby Chaney, in discussion with the author (phone), July 20, 2006.
15. Christine Bleackley, in discussion with the author (phone), February 22, 2007.
16. Norman Magden, "Subversive Scatology and Political Pornography: Funk Film and the Visual Arts," unpublished paper, presented at 2007 Southeastern College Art Conference, Charleston, VA.
17. Berry, Ibid.

CHAPTER 7

Sausage City and Adam's Music

Adam's animation is critically recognized for its pioneering innovation and cosmic imagery. The evolution of sound in his animation is closely entwined with his visual exploration. In numerous discussions, people volunteer that they remember him playing the guitar, seeming to always have it with him, during high school and onward. He was remembered singing and playing at Antioch, sometimes funny tunes, often making them up on the spot. At CalArts, he was known for sitting and playing in the stairwell or outside. He played casually with friends, in one loose "psychedelic rock and roll" ensemble called "The Drugs are Bad," which included George Lockwood and Randle (Randy) Akerson.[1] Deirdre Beckett confirmed that playing the guitar was something her brother did all the time (Figure 7.1). We don't have a record of the breadth of music that he listened to or played; several people mentioned that he played in the style of John Fahey. Music played an important role in his life and was intuitively connected to his thinking in terms of structure and pattern through time.

FIGURE 7.1 Adam with guitar, circa 1976. (Used with permission from Chris Casady.)

His first films, *The Letter* and *Early Animations*, were silent. He enlisted three colleagues to perform J.S. Bach compositions for *Dear Janice*, as discussed earlier. In the spring of 1971, he took a Sound Techniques for Motion Pictures class, covering soundtrack construction, taught by Don Worthen, who oversaw the sound mix for student projects. By 1973, Adam made a step forward in considering the relationship of sound and moving image, keenly aware of the potential for interplay and shared structure. He turned to electronically synthesized music, collaborating with his close peers Carl Stone and Barry Schrader, who composed the scores to *Evolution of the Red Star* and *Heavy-Light*, respectively. They had access to the Buchla 200 through Morton Subotnick, who was involved with the development of that analog audio synthesizer.

Schrader describes the synthesizer as follows: "The Buchla did not have a keyboard, it had a touch tap—it was a plate with a series of touch 'keys' on it which really were moisture sensitive so that when you touched it your finger closed the circuit. But you couldn't *play* it because it was all flat and it wasn't laid out a traditional keyboard way, they were just really ways that you could trigger things or change voltages."[2]

This was before Musical Instrument Digital Interface (MIDI) signals were standardized; they were using an analog synthesizer and an analog tape recording machine. This was then output or "rolled off" to an optical film track and then transferred to a 35-mm magnetic track to be mixed down.[3] Both Stone and Schrader were working with electronic composition and following contemporary ideas of creating soundscapes. Gone were the traditional meters and melodies; these were replaced by experimental form and sound created from electronic circuitry. In *Evolution of the Red Star*, synthesized sound waves drone and pulse, layered to correspond to and compliment the radiating lines and growing complexity within the frame. Electronic tones cascade, rise, and release, following the diving, modulating color forms in *Heavy-Light*.

Adam made *Flesh Flows* immediately after *Heavy-Light*, and for the first time, he created his own sound score, using tape-recorded sounds deftly mixed with the oversight of Worthen. Working in the realm of electroacoustic music, he created a restrained ambient tone by using the sound of running water and recorded choral voices as his source material. It is the most minimal of his soundtracks and perhaps the only thing he created that can be described as such.

Adam, in his synopsis of this work, says, "The sound is intended to encourage a spirit of contemplation on the part of the audience."[4] His soundscape succeeds in doing so, as it builds in intensity with each repeated iteration of the loop (remember, there are three "chapters"), echoing the growing complexity of the optically printed layers. The last incarnation of this journey achieves complete transformation; the minimal sustained note from the CalArts Chorus, or a member of that group, swells over the ambient sound, signaling our arrival at the apex of the experience. Adam has deftly created a sonic space in which images live and evolve and has demonstrated his aptitude for structuring sound with image.

There are no specific sound credits in *Flesh Flows*, however, there is a "Special Thanks to Roberta Friedman and the CalArts Chorus." Friedman was a graduate student in the live action program of the film school, and was active in the art film community in Los Angeles. (Friedmann was one of the founders, with O'Neill, David and Diana Wilson, and others, of the Los Angeles Independent Film Oasis, in 1976.) *Flesh Flows* marks an apex in Adam's independent animation. There is a clear, intuited structure, a balance of technical acuity and human presence, and he has designed a sound score that grounds the piece and gives it depth.

Sausage City came close on the heels of *Flesh Flows*; both films screened in the Humboldt International Film Festival in late February of 1974. Compared with the fluid lines and movement of *Flesh Flows*, and the earlier *Heavy-Light*, this newer film is a regression in terms of image quality and visual cohesion. The sound score ranges from a jazzy tune to sonic exploration and contributes critical structure and focus.

The visual elements and evolving cycles recall the morphing geometric forms of *The Letter* and the organic, rounded shapes in *Dear Janice* (Figure 7.2). *Sausage City* was being developed in parallel to those earlier pieces. As previously noted, in 1974, he wrote that he had been working on *Sausage City* for "three to four years on and off,"[5] and in 1978, he indicated that he had started *Sausage City* in 1968.[6]

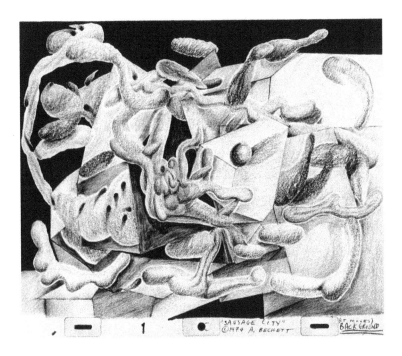

FIGURE 7.2 Black-and-white background image for *Sausage City*, signed and dated. (Used with permission from Beckett's family.)

The opening cycle of *Sausage City* begins simply, as the outline of a rectangular shape fades in. As the cycle builds and repeats, we see that the rectangle evolves from a small square, which grows while rotating. This is the minimal base for the 4-second cycle composed of a sequence of 48 drawings that will build into a cacophonous display. More geometric shapes are added, giving the illusion that the rectangle continues to metamorphose into an ever-expanding variety of polygonal forms. This progresses until the frame is completely filled with a mesmerizing unfolding of what Adam describes in the Canyon Cinema catalog synopsis as a "city of interlocking boxes."

The second movement of his orchestrated visual composition introduces organic, colorful forms—Adam's "sausages"—that move across, in, and out of the implied surface planes of the geometric shapes, changing our perception of these from flat forms into three-dimensional "boxes." These myriad blobs are rendered in color pencil, in contrast to the monochromatic outlines of the planes. As the teeming mass builds, the top background area fills with dark blue, and color is added to some of the boxes, helping to organize the field of movement. As with *Dear Janice*'s fugue-like structure of recursion and change, we are compelled to follow the evolution of a single metamorphosing form and then shift perspective to take in the whole vista of "seething, throbbing, pullulating life."[7] The sound, too, invites taking in the cacophonous whole, then shifting attention to follow a singular thread that catches our ear.

The wild jungle of sound snaps back to the jazzy composition of the opening credits, signaling a change in the cavorting imagery. The camera pulls back, revealing the animation stand's registration system, wooden surface, and the animating drawings, with the numbers at the bottom counting 1–48 and repeating. A character, a man in a hat, enters the frame from the left, as if coming from our "real" space outside of the animated world. He looks at us, turns, and walks into the animation, changing persona as he goes; his head morphs to resemble that of a rather demented Mickey Mouse. He turns back toward us, sticks out his tongue, and extracts a cube from his round nose. As he extends the cube out, it unfolds, filling the frame, so that the scene is now a room with loosely colored walls and a doorway, moving us toward the ending. "THE END" is formed from tumbling geometric shapes, and, with a final accented note from the reeds instrument, the image disappears.

This self-reflexive final segment reveals the space of the animated drawings, a revelation shared by the character, who, while animated, is for a moment complicit in the viewer's reality. It's as if he is making a choice whether to stay with us or escape into the animation. This layering of reality is achieved through careful matting, using a traced outline of the character that is filled with black, isolated on a white background. He shot these

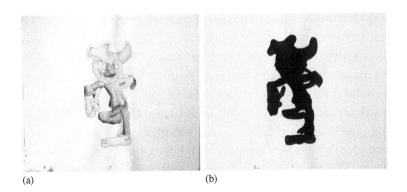

(a)   (b)

FIGURE 7.3   Character at the end of *Sausage City*. (a) Character without background. (b) Matte of character. (Used with permission from Beckett's family.)

black-and-white mattes on high-contrast film, in order to composite the character and the footage of the moving images on the animation stand (Figure 7.3). An unused animation drawing of the character was found with notes and musings written on it, including "cut outs of printed cycles can be glued to cels," a record of him considering matting strategies.

The soundtrack for this work is attributed to a mythical band called "Brillo," "consisting of" Pard (piano), Tiger (guitar), Frisky (drums), Puff (bass), and King (reeds). (The identities of these "cool cats" have evaded my search.) The sound treatment is integral to the piece; here, Adam has moved into the role of conductor and possibly composer. The lively movement of the opening credits appears to be animated to follow the sound of the bouncy jazz composition. In contrast, the music in the body and ending of the film was almost certainly recorded while watching the film, as the musicians responded to visual cues, such as a burst of laughter when a matrix of five circular lights appeared, briefly reflected on the glass of the animation stand. The opening tune returns at the end of the film; however, the performance has a different tempo, as it was being guided by the animation and perhaps with Adam conducting.

In the seconds before images appear, we hear him instruct the musicians, saying "Alright. Look at Puff," which resulted in howls of laughter from the assembled musicians. (A close listen makes me suspect that he actually said "Butt" and not "Puff" and may have been referring to himself.) He then very seriously and purposefully said, "Take *four*." The jazzy tune plays through the opening credits and ends with a final accented note, leaving silence and an empty screen for a moment before the animation proper begins. The sound that then ensues is an improvised soundscape using voice and instruments played in nontraditional ways. The process was somewhere between Foley sound, free jazz style, and abstract accompaniment, as the group riffed off of the cacophony of visuals. We hear a voice in the background, speaking nonsensically, "booda-booda-booda," and a strummed or bowed string, making ascending notes. The sound is a raucous mix of voices and jumbled improvisation on the instruments, with the density and volume building and diminishing; sonic elements rise to the forefront and recede into the chaos. It underscores the wackiness of the visual experience. The ending, as noted, leads back to the more organized jazz tune, as the animation resolves with the entry of the character. While the tune's composition is the same, it is not as tightly executed as if the band members were struggling to become cohesive again after such a meandering romp of improvisation, using the animation as a cue.

With *Flesh Flows* and *Sausage City* being completed and released so close together, it may be a mistake to think that one sound score was created before the other. His experience of recording the jazzy and raucous "Brillo" could have led to his work with the Chorus, a more controlled and focused recording—or the opposite could have occurred, moving from control to chaos. Clues may be on the actual mag tracks or written on the film cans that hold them. What is obvious, and important, is that Adam at this point has a keen awareness of the connection between audio and image and also has the skill and confidence to produce the sound for his work.

In the spring of 1975, Adam returned to CalArts, not as a student but as an instructor. He was asked to teach an optical printing and an animation class, filling a void left by Pat O'Neill, who didn't return, owing to health issues. Adam deftly devised a collaborative project that would involve both classes, teaching them how to use the equipment, while at the same time creating an animated film. Many of the students with whom Adam worked would later become notable artists, especially in the visual effects industry, including Robert Luttrell, Thomas Edmon, Peter Kuran, and John Scheele. Randy Akerson went on to have an extensive career as a sound editor. Mark Kirkland entered the animation industry and has directed numerous episodes of *The Simpsons*. David Wilson, with his wife Diana, founded the extraordinary Museum of Jurassic Technology.

Adam's innovative use of the optical printer, involving an inconceivable number of layers and passes through the printer, would have been formidable for the class, and Adam would not have been eager to divulge his process. He had learned how to use the optical printer from O'Neill and turned to that experience for this class. The resulting film gave a nod to the masterful earlier work of O'Neill (particularly his *7362*, from 1967), with colorful mirrored images that are flipped and repeated (Figure 7.4).

Titled *Kitsch in Synch*, this film featured an original soundtrack. Rather than using prerecorded music, he enlisted some of his students—and probably a few who weren't—to improvise with voice and instruments, led by Adam. They did this before starting to animate, as the sound would determine the timing and structure of the piece. They recorded a wacky, rhythmic vocal chant that was altered during the mix, making the voices high and childlike and often humorous. The track was sped up, adding to the frantic feel in some places and further obscuring the source of the sounds. The voices start fairly simply, chanting "BUBUBABU" (Adam's word from his Canyon Cinema description). This builds in intensity, accelerates into mayhem, and then stops, only to repeat with variations. A more meditative segment

FIGURE 7.4 Still from *Kitsch in Synch*; paper cutout images, colored and mirrored on the optical printer. (Used with permission from the iotaCenter.)

of audio breaks the sound riot twice, accompanied by a change in the visual pace and composition as well. These respites feature a sitar-like strumming that is probably Adam playing the banjo. He is joined by a harmonica—or it may have been a clarinet played by Mark Kirkland[8]—in one section, although due to the mix it, too, sounds much higher-pitched, and faster. As confirmed by his friend and collaborator Carl Stone, the banjo was another instrument that Adam loved to play.[9]

When the track is slowed down to approximate normal pitch and speed, the voices are chaotic and nonsensical, and seem to be following an irregular beat provided by the striking of a drum or similar object, as well as prompted by a conductor. Even in the "normalized" version, there are high-pitched voices mixed underneath, indicating that the soundtrack, like the moving image, had layered iterations as well. It is a performed cycle that is repeating with change. The results proved so innovative and infectious that the film won an award for best sound score at Cinemedia VI in 1975.

Once the audio was recorded and ready, an exposure sheet was made to mark the beats and changes and to provide the map for creating and composing the visual components. Students in the animation class cut shapes out of black-and-white paper and animated these on a lightbox under the animation camera. As Peter Kuran recalls, "most of the less creative aspects would be done in the animation camera and then the class would take the animation and do optical printing with it—that's where most of the creativity actually wound up."[10] The animation of the cutout paper became the primary source material for an array of optical processes. Vibrant, pure color was added to the shapes, and mirrored images were layered over top of each other, with the replicas often being a different color. A square on one side that was bright blue might be mirrored as orange.

There was a variety of images, including geometric shapes, organic Matisse-like forms, jagged lightning bolts, the silhouette of a steer head, a crocodile or dinosaur head, stars, a swan, Saturn or perhaps an unidentified flying object, and a running figure. At one point, there are shapes with round holes punched out, and then, the paper dots from the holes animate and form the mirrored phrase, "Adam is a...," with the final word obscured. Most of these forms go by quickly, used as shape, color, and texture, devoid of narrative.

Just over 3 minutes into the film (which has a running time of 5 minutes and 40 seconds), the images become denser, and more representational forms appear, such as the head of the steer and the swan. Photographic forms are beneath the shifting, pulsing mass, discernible just enough to add intrigue. The image of a rider on a horse, printed as a silhouette, was from a film of George Lockwood on a horse, contributed by Randy Akerson (Figure 7.5).

FIGURE 7.5   Still from *Kitsch in Synch*; layered footage with the rider on a horse. (Used with permission from the iotaCenter.)

Lockwood notes the discontent arising from Adam's making of a film with students as the labor. He recalls, "Adam had this thing he wanted to do so he just used this class to get his thing done. So I suppose that if you were really into printing you would have been able to pick up on what he was doing... but if you were doing other things you just didn't get it. But basically he told everyone in the class to bring me some outtakes, bring me some film."[11] And Akerson brought in footage of Lockwood on the horse. The film was screened as Adam's animation, and in truth, he was what we now understand as the producer and director and one of the numerous people who worked on the animation, music, and opticals. The students' names were included in the opening credits but optically printed with so many phased layers that the names were practically impossible to read, which of course added to the discontent of the contributors. He compromised by adding the names in a straightforward manner at the end of the film.

Students had conflicting reactions to Adam as a teacher. Some were wary of him, and others saw him as patient, knowledgeable, and helpful. Gar LaSalle, who was in the class, while also pursuing a successful career as a medical doctor, recalls that Adam showed a lot of films that used optical printing, to give the students a variety of approaches. He also remembers that he had a gentle way of teasing students, as he did when one student put the film in the printer backward. He alluded to a cartoon, where the character had stuffed his suitcase and struggled to shut it and, once it was closed, noticed the end of a tie sticking out. He got a pair of scissors and cut the end off to fix the problem.[12] Because of the foibles of memory, with its compressed and often confused time, it is hard to discern if the wariness is from later experiences with Adam or from the events that occurred during the class. Several former students and colleagues commented on his ability to detect weak spots in people and that he sometimes seemed to get pleasure out of targeting those spots.

Once released, *Kitsch in Synch* was an immediate hit. Diana Wilson distinctly remembers that she first saw this film while at Kathy Rose's house and that she was stunned and impressed by it. While acknowledging that it was a class project, with lots of people contributing to it, she pointed out that "Somehow it was Adam's dementia that came through." The film that they saw at Rose's house was probably not the final completed film, as he worked on it for a while, creating, as Wilson described, "many manifestations."[13]

As with prior films, Adam submitted *Kitsch in Synch* to films festivals, not as a collaborative work but as an animation that he directed, which was, technically, accurate. In an article reviewing the screening of the annual Cinemedia VI student film competition, Kevin Thomas wrote, "In 'Kitsch in Synch,' Adam Beckett, one of CalArts' most talented students, has again created a dazzling abstract work incorporating pop art imagery and a vibrant, freewheeling score."[14] While it was a film created by students, under the guidance of a teaching assistant, technically, Adam was not a student at this time.

The film was awarded $250 in the competition, possibly adding to the irritation felt by his reluctant collaborators.[15] The credits include the students, as noted, and that it was made at CalArts, but as a presentation of Adam's studio, Infinite Animation, Ltd.

It was the last film that Adam submitted to festivals.

While his animations were doing well in the world, there was always the pressure to produce the next one. Adam was navigating changes in his personal life, and without a steady compass. His father was a chronic alcoholic and a volatile figure in Adam's life, yet someone whose approval he seemed to need. A close friend recalls that one summer (it would have been 1973 or 1974), Adam drove to Kansas City to retrieve his father, who was there on a binge. At some point in 1974, Rose had moved into Adam's tiny house in Val Verde and quickly realized that it was impossible for two adults and a dog to share the limited, untidy space. She didn't stay long. They were both developing professionals and under pressure to succeed. The selection of three of his animations for inclusion in the "Animation" program at the Whitney caused a strain between them, as did the winning of the gold Hugo award by Rose and the bronze by Adam. There is a CalArts press photo of her with the treasured award, dated November 28, 1974, among Adam's many papers. On the back, he has written "IT'S OVER" three times in black marker, with the date "5/25/75" and in pencil "It is over the years of Rose." They had, according to Rose, actually broken up in late 1974, but he was slow to accept it; she returned to New York City in the fall of 1975.

Adam received a letter in January of 1975 from animator Kathleen Laughlin, who was then teaching with Suzan Pitt at the Minneapolis College of Art and Design. She was inquiring about his technique and also asked if he might be interested in teaching.[16] His response (which he may have never sent, or perhaps retyped, keeping the draft) is revealing. He writes that he rereads her letter from "time to time to cheer myself up" and that while he has taken over O'Neill's classes, "I don't have the world's greatest personality for teaching, tending to fly off the handle at myself enough as it is when I encounter stupidity on my part, but I'm learning, I hope, how to be patient, etc."

Perhaps more critically, Adam cited his primary hesitation being that he was "really plugged into the fancy technical apparatus" and that equipment is available primarily in cities such as Los Angeles and New York City. "That AFI film depends entirely on a good optical printer and I intend to finish it before I do anything else."[17] After this declaration, he unexpectedly added, "Howsomeever it has increasingly been my desire or self delusion that these machines are just a passing phase and soon, someday, I will leave the hurly-burly of fixed pin-registration and sit down at my drawing board again." His films had been met with success, but here, we see doubt and perhaps a desire to return to the simplicity of the drawn image.

BIBLIOGRAPHY

American Federation of the Arts. 1976. *New American Filmmakers: Selections from the Whitney Museum of American Art Film Program*. New York: American Federation of the Arts.

Beckett, Adam. 1976. *Canyon Cinema Cooperative Catalog #4*, Canyon Cinema. San Francisco, CA: Warren's Waller Press.

Beckett, Adam. *Letter to Terry Kemper.* Frances Mulhall Achilles Library, Archives, New York: Whitney Museum of American Art, NY. John Hanhardt artist files, Box 3, Adam Beckett folder.

Los Angeles Times. "Cinemedia Top Films to be Screened at Museum," *Los Angeles Times*, September 6, 1975.

Thomas, Kevin. "46 Student Films in Spotlight," *Los Angeles Times,* September 12, 1975.

ENDNOTES

[1] George Lockwood, in discussion with the author (phone), October 12, 2005.

[2] Barry Schrader, interview by the author, October 1, 2004.

[3] Ibid.

[4] Beckett's description in the "New American Filmmakers: Selections from the Whitney Museum of American Art Film Program" 1976 catalog, American Federation of the Arts, 75.

5 Adam Beckett in letter to Jerry Kemper, August 6, 1974, on CalArts stationary. Frances Mulhall Achilles Library, Archives, Whitney Museum of Art, NY. Series: John Hanhardt artist files, Box 3, Folder Beckett, Adam.

6 Adam Beckett, personal letter to Jim Trainor (then in high school), dated May 3, 1978 (at 3:10am). Courtesy of Jim Trainor.

7 Beckett synopsis for *Sausage City, Canyon Cinema Cooperative Catalog #4*. 1976, Canyon Cinema, Inc., San Francisco, CA: Warren's Waller Press, 17.

8 Carl Stone, interview by the author, March 5, 2003.

9 Mark Kirkland, message to author, March 12, 2012.

10 Peter Kuran, in discussion with the author (phone) July 23, 2004.

11 Lockwood, Ibid.

12 Gar LaSalle, in discussion with the author (phone), February 16, 2004.

13 Diana Wilson, interview by the author, March 17, 2005.

14 Kevin Thomas, "Student Films in Spotlight," *Los Angeles Times*, September 12, 1975, 102. https://www.newspapers.com/image/165521376.

15 "Cinemedia Top Films to Be Screened at Museum," *Los Angeles Times*, September 6, 1975, 42. https://www.newspapers.com/image/165277544.

16 Letter from Kathleen Laughlin to Beckett, dated January 19, 1975.

17 Letter to Kathleen Laughlin from Beckett, dated February 12, 1975.

CHAPTER 8

Bridging Art and Effects

A New Generation Emerges

A DAM DID NOT RETURN to the graduate program at CalArts. He was a freelance animator navigating the changing economic and cultural landscape of the mid-1970s. The decade's economy warranted the label "The Great Inflation," with the years 1973 through 1975 marked by economic recession. The stock market was unstable; unemployment rose to just over 8% in January of 1975; and the oil crisis of 1973 resulted in lines of cars vying for position at the gas pumps. The optimism expressed in the bright graphics of the 1960s had long faded. Adam came from a well-to-do family, so presumably, it was choice and not circumstance that had placed him in a tiny shack in Val Verde. Even so, he could not have been immune to the economic struggles around him.

The art board that prominently features Libby Chaney's name illustrates, literally, his musings on his future and recent personal events, giving valuable clues to his state of mind during this time (Figure 8.1). It is covered with drawings and writing and is a

FIGURE 8.1 Art board featuring "Libby Chaney" and his questions for the future. The results of his I-Ching throw are on the left, under the drawing of the penny. (Used with permission from Beckett's family.)

fascinating piece to contemplate. He is throwing the I-Ching and asking "Is 1976 'A' lucky year?" Next to this, he has written "SO IT WOULD APPEAR" and a list of eight possible reasons, the first being "BILLS ARE PAID." The second is "DEATH IS FACED," and the last is "WORK." Rose confirmed the notations of the I-Ching and, with a quick read, interpreted the answer as "moving into nourishment."[1] While she recalled that this was a time of emotional turmoil for Adam, his text and doodles express an overall optimism. Perhaps, this springs from the I-Ching results or a new infatuation with Chaney. There is lyrical writing about finding a pony's bones in the mountains, which were deer bones, as Chaney recalled. He is also wrestling with pragmatism, writing "the time has come to choose between reality and fantasy" and has an ongoing word play between "LIFE" and "JOB," asking questions such as "JOB IS REAL LIFE?" and "LIFE IS REAL JOB?"

While Adam's films were successful in festivals and continuing to gain recognition, it was increasingly obvious by late 1974 that independent animation was not a sustainable occupation. Film rental costs were usually based on the length of the film, which for his work meant little profit after the cost of striking additional prints and shipping. The invoice to Ron Epple at Picture Start lists the rental at $10 per film. Canyon Cinema Cooperative rental prices in the 1976 catalog (the year he joined) were $18.50 for *Evolution of the Red Star*, $18 for *Flesh Flows*, $14 for *Heavy-Light*, and $10 each for *Kitsch in Sync* and *Sausage City*. *Dear Janice* was not listed; however it can be found in the original artwork he provided for the catalog, with "due out soon" written in very small letters (Figure 8.2). The filmmakers' agreement states that the artist sets the rate but advises that the usual rate is between $1 and $2 per minute of running time. The filmmaker received 60% of the rental fees. Adam's Canyon Cinema records reflect that he earned $283.50 in rental fees in 1977 and that it cost $8 to be a member of the cooperative.[2] His record also provides a valuable document of where his work screened. These venues included Ohio University in Athens, University of Arkansas in Fayetteville, San Francisco Museum of Art, and Grand Rapids Art Museum, and several films were included in Mike Getz's Underground Cinema screening tours. The American Federation of the Arts 1976 catalog carried three titles: *Evolution of the Red Star* ($18.50 for rental and $180 to buy), *Flesh Flows* ($18 rental and $110 to buy), and *Sausage City* ($12 rental and $90 to buy).

On the East Coast, Kathy Rose and Deanna Morse, along with many other independent animators, contributed animated segments to *Sesame Street* as a way to support themselves through their work. While Adam may have had other freelance projects,

FIGURE 8.2 Adam's negative film of his page for the 1976 Canyon Cinema Cooperative Catalog. (Used with permission from Beckett's family.)

we know that he contributed to John and Faith Hubley's *Everybody Rides the Carousel* in early 1975. He was one of two young experimental animators added to the team that included, among others, Michael Sporn, Bill Littlejohn, Art Babbit, the Hubleys, and Earl James. Michael Sporn, in his informative animation blog—or

"Splog"—shared what may be the only recollection of Adam's contribution to the film, noting that he did a scene "wherein office furniture floated about in a very complicated surreal cycle."[3] He also animated a street scene, where a car rolls by; an unfinished discarded frame from that sequence stands out from his other animation drawings as it is clearly connected to a narrative (Figure 8.3).

Adam refined his bag of alchemical visual tricks in his experiments for *Knotte Grosse*, the film he was determined to finish. This collection of tests demonstrates a breakthrough in technical acuity and controlled orchestration of moving shapes on the screen. He was using 35-mm film to achieve higher detail and resolution. The restored elements of this work include two sections, dated 1974 and April 1975, respectively. Also labeled "Examples," it reads like a demo reel of visual effects exercises and may have been used for that purpose. Adam would have, of course, been familiar with John Whitney Sr.'s *Catalog* from 1961 and other motion graphics that Whitney created on equipment that he devised.

FIGURE 8.3 Unfinished animation drawing for the Hubley's *Everybody Loves the Carousel*. (Used with permission from Beckett's family.)

Initially, these images appear to be computer generated; however, that would have been difficult without access to a facility, computers were not readily available. He would be aware of computer animation through festivals and local screenings. John Stehura's *Cibernetic 5.2* played alongside Adam's work at the Theatre Vanguard in 1973 and was discussed in Youngblood's *Expanded Cinema*. The computer-generated *Metathesis* and *Metamorphosis* by Lillian Schwartz and Ken Knowlton were in the "Animation" program at the Whitney in the winter of 1974. Also in 1974, his classmate Larry Cuba, with Gary Imhoff, released *First Fig*, an abstract animation made using the computer equipment in an unofficial capacity at Jet Propulsion Laboratory. Adam's complex logic operations on the optical printer, especially in *Knotte Grosse*, were his own form of coding. This film demonstrates a significant step forward in the ability to control the placement and movement of the image elements. This, and the fact that he is shooting on 35-mm film, suggests that he would not have been on the CalArts optical printer but had gained access to Robert Abel's studio or elsewhere. O'Neill recalls that when Adam was no longer a student and needed access to equipment he used O'Neill's optical printer a few times.[4]

With *Knotte Grosse*, one becomes keenly aware of Adam's daunting mathematical ability. It is a visual manifestation of sets and supersets, with recursive moving groups of objects iterated temporally and spatially, resulting in new, complex and intricate patterns. The primary pattern of moving objects would be repeated in multiples, organizing into a matrix that filled the picture plane with synchronized movement. The whole was a reflection of the part, creating complexity from simplicity. Adam's system was on a parallel trajectory with the concurrently emerging theoretical work of mathematician Benoit Mandelbrot. *Fractals: Form, Chance and Dimension* was published in September of 1977, 2 years after Adam's experiments.

The first section on the restored film is dated 1974 and begins with what appears to be vertical lines that lean and rotate, reminiscent, as noted by some, of Oskar Fischinger's animated cigarettes in *Muratti Privat* (1935). Adam's lines are actually made of tiny squares. The incremental shifting of the individual squares creates the movement. The base square rotates from a fixed position, functioning as a pivot point for the squares connected to it. The next square rotates and moves in the x and y directions, around the pivot, with each square mimicking the one before. In this way, he created images whose movement had a logic that resonated with computer programming, but he used drawn images and carefully controlled movements on the optical printer.

In another section, he used a similar system with different source images, which generated radically different patterns. The images were loosely drawn cubes in sets of four, each individual cube variously positioned and colored. A three-dimensional space is implied, as they appear to move behind or in front of each other. There are numerous variations of these sets of moving cubes, and the sets themselves move, combining and overlapping each other. These patterns are then used as a source, repeated to generate multiples, smaller in scale to fit the space, their combinations, again creating new patterns. That, too, is duplicated and offset in movement, repeating this self-generating process until the individual original sets of cubes are indiscernible, mere points on a screen. They are tiny components of moving, fractal images (Figure 8.4). As the ensemble of iterations combines, it briefly resembles a snowflake-like pattern (Figure 8.5). As with his earlier cycles, our attention follows the parts and then shifts to see the whole.

Adam continued this iterative process in the second part of the film, made in 1975. Here, the letters "A," "B," and "C" are created with mattes, and the undulating patterns appear inside of the forms. While this seems like a practical way—and it was—to organize and keep track of the patterns, much like using variables in an algorithm, it isn't a coincidence that, during this time, the logo for the ABC television network was a primary project of Robert Abel and Associates.

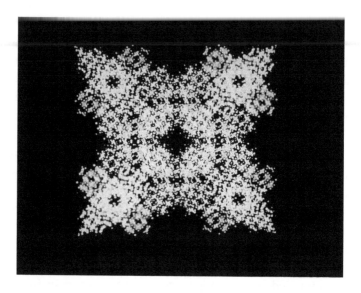

FIGURE 8.4   Still frame from a *Knotte Grosse* experiment that generates patterns resembling a snowflake. (Used with permission from the iotaCenter.)

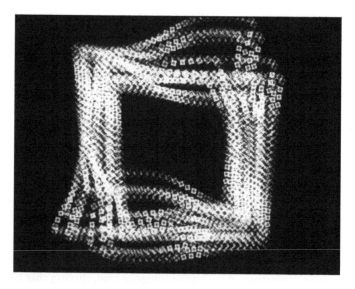

FIGURE 8.5   Still frame from one of the *Knotte Grosse* experiments. (Used with permission from the iotaCenter.)

Dave Berry remembers Adam creating these "stunning looking graphics" and confirms that Adam used the equipment at Abel's studio, where he also extended his knowledge of mathematical applications.[5] This would have been fertile ground owing to his proclivity toward math. By adding a date to this section, Adam differentiated it from the work done in 1974; it also helps to determine when he was at Abel's studio. Richard Taylor, who was at Abel's, doesn't remember a film called "Knotte Grosse" but confirms that the studio had a computer-controlled camera and two horizontal tracks that were used to do motion effects, and they had Oxberry stands, which they called the "down-shooters." Adam was working on the backlit Oxberry that had the capability to make controlled and repeated movements.[6]

George Lockwood has a vivid memory of *Knotte Grosse*, specifically the ABC logo test that Adam created. He indicates that the matrix of squares may not have been intentional and that Adam was aiming for a seamless array of movement. The existing equipment wasn't yet accurate enough.[7] The short segments following the ABC experiments, however, become more seamless. These show a grid of undulating movement across the screen and geometric, quilt-like patterns.

Needing more regular access to advanced equipment, Adam wrote a proposal to CalArts (no specific recipient), dated November 3, 1975, suggesting that he be allowed the use of the Oxberry animation stand and the optical printer equipment in exchange for 35-mm capability for the Oxberry. He would supply "35 mm movements and a 400 ft magazine."[8] The typed proposal was found among his personal papers; he may have never sent it or possibly sent a different version. It reflects that things had changed for him at CalArts; he no longer could use the facilities there, at least not with sanctioned access; however, he was there as late as 1976.[9] He did the optical printing work on *Angie* (1976) by Deirdre Cowden, a student who was working on this homage to the Rolling Stones.

Adam's ingenuity on the animation camera and optical printer was a perfect bridge to the visual effects industry. His mentor, Jules Engel, had links to the broadcast and film industries through his impressive career of work in animation at Disney, United Productions of America (UPA), and Format Films, as well as in live action film. He did a few projects through Westheimer Studios, a notable film graphics house in Hollywood, run by Joe Westheimer. Adam's colleague and teacher Pat O'Neill had launched his Lookout Mountain studio to apply his optical printing mastery to commercial projects for hire that would in turn support his art. O'Neill and Robert Abel made *By the Sea* in 1963 while they were college mates at the University of California, Los Angeles (UCLA). The industry and arts in Los Angeles had numerous points of overlap.

Abel, Dave Stewart, and Con Pederson, founded Robert Abel and Associates in 1971. Pederson, a seasoned professional in effects, had supervised the special photographic effects on *2001: A Space Odyssey* (1968) and had brought his technical and artistic expertise. Taylor, who was directing and creating effects at Robert Abel and Associates, met Adam through their mutual friend O'Neill. Abel's studio, in particular, was on a mission to develop new techniques and technologies to create novel images that reflected the color and shape of contemporary culture on broadcast media.

Taylor was impressed with Adam's films, his advanced technical acuity, and his inherent drive to experiment, so he enlisted Adam at Abel's for several projects. They were working on broadcast graphics for the ABC network, as noted earlier, and recognized potential in Adam's exquisite multiple-pass printing technique. Taylor recalls, "We were just experimenting, really, with different kinds of treatments that we might do using that effect that he had developed."[10]

According to Taylor, Adam contributed to an Abel studio's Maybelline mascara commercial that aired in 1976. The spot was fairly psychedelic, as consistent with both Adam and Taylor's graphic style and experience. Taylor had worked, previous to his graduate studies at the University of Southern California, with the group Rainbow Jam, creating light shows for many of the prominent rock groups from the late 1960s and early 1970s. In the commercial for Maybelline, the focus becomes the model's eyelashes, and as he describes it: "When she opened her eye, her eyelashes started spraying off towards you and became these kind of rainbow fans of color that just flowed by. Flowed off of her eyes."[11] The equipment they were using at that time was not digital. They relied heavily on the Oxberry animation stands, a horizontal track for the camera, and analog computer-controlled camera motion, so that camera moves could be controlled and accurately repeated or repeated with an offset.

Similar efforts to push technology and innovate for advanced moving images were developing elsewhere; a new generation of visual effects artists was emerging. Richard Edlund, having learned the ropes at Westheimer Studios, creating titles, commercials, and optical effects, joined Abel's studio in 1973 around the same time as Taylor.[12] Doug Trumbull, who had worked with Pederson on *2001*, had just set up a studio, Future General Corporation. John Dykstra worked with him as they filmed *Silent Running* (1972), a postapocalyptic science fiction movie, taking place in outer space. It was directed by 29-year-old Trumbull. Pederson, Abel, Taylor, Edlund, Dykstra, and Trumbull were key figures in the amazing lineage of visual effects artistry and invention that was emerging. Adam, with numerous CalArts classmates, soon became woven into that legacy.

Talent was being recruited to set up a new visual effects facility, in a Van Nuys warehouse, in the summer of 1975. The project was a feature film, one that was initially thought to be a low-budget, nonunion cowboy movie set in outer space. The director, George Lucas, had described this future project as a "space opera,"[13] situating it in an established subgenre of science fiction. Initially called "*The Star Wars*," it would be released less than 2 years after the effects studio was up and running.

Some who heard rumblings of this potential project assumed that it was going to be more of a B-level, cult space-cowboy film. Science fiction films were by no means novel. There had been a few recent movies set in outer space: *2001: A Space Odyssey* (1968), *THX 1138* (1971, directed by Lucas), *Silent Running* (1972), *Dark Star* (1974), and *Logan's Run* (1976). *Star Wars* was working outside of the big studio system, which may have been the source of some of the doubt. Tom Barron, who knew Adam from CalArts and worked at Abel's (and later created his own company, Image G), recalls that this production, in contrast to the Hollywood model, was "cheap and fast." At some point, Lucas, who was in England, where the actors were being filmed, "sort of had an epiphany that this was going to be a big important movie."[14] It would not be a drama primarily situated inside of spaceships or with feet on the ground of a fictional planet. Lucas's project was an action movie with aerial battles similar to those filmed during World War II, but the heroic fights that his team would need to film were in a galaxy far, far away. Choreographing and shooting this action would require considerable technical innovation. Various teams would need to collaborate to pull off meshing dynamic motion images of models, laser beams, and explosions with live action footage of actors and sets.

The "special photographic effects" in the feature film industry had not experienced forward development in several decades. In the past, the traditional creation of special effects relied on stop-motion animation techniques, in-camera compositing, front projection, matte paintings, and compositing on the optical printer. Variations of chroma keying were done as well, with actors shot on white backgrounds or with areas blacked out to be later filled with footage. Film was composited using garbage and traveling mattes to control what was being exposed on the film. Blue screen was first used in 1959 in the making of *Ben Hur*, with improvements pioneered by Petro Vlahos, for which he won an Oscar in 1964. By 1975, many of the early effects specialists were retired. This new generation would need to dig into the past, while at the same time pioneering new technologies.

The making of *Star Wars* set into motion a precipitous gathering of unique talents, including Adam. Those close to it knew that it wasn't just another sci-fi film; there was an undercurrent of challenge and discovery that inspired passion. Robert Blalack, also from CalArts, had started his own company, Praxis Film Works, by 1975. He was brought in to help set up the optical department, where images would be composited. In considering Adam's—and his—mindset at that time, Blalack wrote, "A few of us were burning to realize what we felt was a new language of film, like prospecting for gold in the soul. If you could get there first, you'd be able to touch people where it counts, open doors that would never be closed thereafter. Like some of us, he ate, slept and lived the obsession."[15]

John Dykstra was brought on board to supervise special photographic effects. Richard Edlund left Abel studios to be the first cameraman for the miniature and optical effects unit. He, along with Blalack, played an integral role in designing the photographic system, which would be essential to successful effects strategies such as matting and shooting on a blue screen set to seamlessly combine live action and effects elements, including animation. Edlund researched and gleaned as much as he could from the "old masters," interviewing them to see what he could learn. With this perspective, he sought out people who had the vision and ingenuity to become the new generation of effects wizards, while also seeking equipment and technologies from which to conjure the numerous illusions that they would be tasked with creating. Through his recommendation, Adam was brought on board to head the animation and rotoscoping department.

The degree of innovation, repurposing, and reconfiguring of equipment that was required to create the various special and visual effects cannot be overstated. One piece of equipment, now known as the Anderson Printer, was hunted down by Edlund, who contacted Harry Anderson, an optical effects and titles specialist from the earlier days of film. Anderson's studio had been on the Paramount lot, and it was there that Edlund found the dust-covered setup in an upstairs space—it had last been used for the 1956 film *The Ten Commandments*. In fact, as Edlund vividly recalls, "The last camera reports written up for *The Ten Commandments* was still sitting right next to the camera. So, the guy shot the test element for *The Ten Commandments* and then walked out of the room and closed the door and nobody had gone back there. Or there was no evidence of them there."[16]

Lucas purchased the equipment. Edlund recounts the acquisition of various elements that would become integral to the next nearly two decades of Industrial Light & Magic's visual effects.

> ... we had 2 or 3 roto benches, we got 2 roto benches, at least 2 other Bell and Howell cameras, countless VistaVision movements. I mean there were negative and positive movements—there were 6 movements for Robbie's printer. Plus, VistaVision movements for the roto cameras.[17]

Blalack, at Praxis, had the equipment that John Dykstra believed would solve some of their problems. Blalack explains,

> I bought the Butler-Glouner 4 perf optical printer from CalArts. Larry Butler and Don Glouner were old optical effects guys from way back. They built the printer specifically for blue screen composites for *Marooned*. They were at the forefront of opticals at the time: it was one of the first, if not the first printer to use stepper motors. I used it for some TV spots and feature work. I met John Dykstra when he was working at Doug Trumbull's effects studio. ... When he got *Star Wars*, he asked me to come in and bring the optical printer.[18]

The printer had to be updated to run 35 mm movie film in VistaVision format, orienting the film frame horizontally, in effect making the frame twice the size of 35 mm. This also meant that each frame had eight perforations that ran along the top and bottom of each frame, as opposed to four perforations along each side. Edlund recalls the gymnastics of creating effects by using existing, reconfigured equipment, as he explains the process of setting up the rotoscoping bench.

> So I had to plop the cameras on the side and figure out mirror systems so that cameras could shoot them and they were backlit. ... You'd project through the camera, through these mirrors, and then you'd trace out where the ship was going, in what direction, and then you'd have to figure out the angle and the timing of the lasers and the vector of the ship because it's moving, and the dynamics of all this—we were in the analog world![19]

Perhaps, the most legendary, integral piece of equipment developed for the film was the Dykstraflex, which evolved from the experiments of Dykstra and the electronics of Alvah Miller and Jerry Jeffress. It was the ultimate motion controlled camera, with the ability to tilt on all axes, swing, pan, crane, and move forward and back, all in computer-programmed (via knobs, not keyboard) movements that could be precisely repeated. This made possible the numerous action shots of the various spaceships; the camera whizzed past them, creating the illusion of objects flying through space. These were usually shot on a blue screen stage, creating the need for numerous mattes and color spill correction—work done in Adam's department.

Adam had a love for the project, as he knew more about science fiction than most people, having been an ardent reader and collector of the genre from his early years. Berry recalled, "He knew all the sources, the derivations of everything that Lucas put in *Star Wars*. He had this huge science fiction library in his house, all the classics and the modern stuff." Adam acknowledged his obsession in an interview by Paul Mandell for *Cinefantastique*, noting that in his early years, he had collected about 2000 science fiction books.[20]

Adam also had access to a stable of extremely capable, innovative artists through his colleagues at CalArts. Chris Casady and Byron Werner worked on the night shift to assist with the rotoscoping. Peter Kuran and Mike Ross, former students who contributed to *Kitsch in Synch*, joined Adam during the day, as did Diana Wilson and Jonathan Seay. Berry worked in the stage area where models were shot and then migrated to the optical department and the night shift. None of them had worked on a feature film before; most were fresh out of CalArts. Werner recalls, "We had no idea that *Star Wars* was going to be this big. We thought it was going to be a little cult film with the sci-fi people. ... And you know, had no idea, *no* idea."[21]

The effects facility that housed the various departments was a warehouse, with some of the walls unfinished. The department as a whole would animate effects, such as lasers, and create mattes, rotoscope actual film footage, and clean up backgrounds, all to make possible the fusion of real and special visual effects. The models of the spaceships were shot against a blue screen background, and if the models were near that blue surface, there would be color "spill"; their shiny curved surfaces would reflect the blue of the screen and cast a white light on the blue background. The supports that held the models had to be removed. Numerous mattes had to be drawn to correct these situations.

According to Casady, Adam and the rotoscope team spent many of the first months largely on research and development. They realized that an assembly line system had to be worked out, so they figured out where production was slowing down and where more people would be needed to get the job done within the tight production schedule. A primary slowdown was matte making, so they decided to bring in people at night to work on the matting—a tedious job that could be relegated to "grunts," as Casady put it.[22] Also, the days in the valley were hot, especially for those working under stage or camera lighting. Even though it was not the most exciting job and only paid $3 an hour, he became part of the rotoscope team that became known as the "bozos." This label was co-opted from pop culture but also referenced the equipment that they had inherited from *The Ten Commandments*. Casady described this as a "'Frankensteined' machine" called the Bozotron. It was a slanted light table with rear projection, enabling the artist to draw in direct reference to the projected film image when creating mattes or effects.

The tremendous amount of work to be done, on a tight schedule, required that some of the effects and animation be outsourced. Adam, in his *Cinefantastique* interview, noted that the laser beams of the laser swords were created at VanDerVeer Photo Effects, while the red bullets, or blaster bolts, were animated by Nina Saxon, a recent UCLA graduate who was working at Modern Film Effects and who later opened her own studio. A critical piece of animation, and the only piece created on a digital computer, was given to Larry Cuba, another CalArts alumni who used the computer facilities at the University of Illinois at Chicago and the GRASS (GRAphics Symbiosis System) programming language developed by Tom DeFanti. The scene was the visualization of the Death Star that was studied in the briefing room, as the Rebel fighters strategized for battle.

Adam explained rotoscoping, a primary task of his department.

Rotoscoping is a process that gives you the capacity of making artwork that precisely matches an existing image on film. The actual process involves a camera/projector unit that enables you to project an existing image and to photograph artwork traced from that image. We had two separate rotoscope units for *Star Wars*. One projected the image from the bottom off the mirrors onto the underside of a sheet of paper or cel, which meant that we had to use translucent or transparent materials. The other camera projected from above directly down onto the art surface, which meant that the image was visible even if we used opaque art materials. The essential gist of rotoscoping is it that it enables one to project and re-photograph repeatedly.[23]

While the first rotoscope setup was used as far back as 1925, the second one was devised by Doug Barnett and was referred to by Werner as the Barnett-o-matic. Adam described it as an instrument that was:

... complete with foot-controlled platen, and exposure controlled in one-twelfth stop increments via a capping shutter. One feature or lack thereof was that we had no camera movement or artwork movement mechanisms. In one shot a planet with a subtle "east to west" motion required a rather exact matte. Several unsuccessful ones were made using *animated artwork* which is a little like bailing out your bathtub with a teaspoon. Finally we taped an engineer's scale from the machine shop down and did the pan on one piece of artwork looking through a magnifier at the one-hundredth inch scale, which worked the first time.[24]

Adam initially thought—and hoped—that his animation wizardry would be useful to create explosions and special effects similar to previous movies and assumed that this type of effect would be a significant part of the action in *Star Wars*. He had, after all, created atmospheric, ethereal imagery, not unlike smoke or colored flames in his films *Heavy-Light* and *Flesh Flows*. George Lockwood agreed that this was a logical project for Adam's talent. "It was a place where the linear, very normal kind of storytelling movie intersected with an abstract imaging in a very specific place and way, and you could see how somebody who was into abstract imagery would really latch onto it."[25] It was soon apparent that he and his crew would be doing more practical and less exotic kind of work.

Colleagues from that time recall Adam's interest in creating animated explosions and his disappointment when that didn't happen. In *Cinefantastique*, Adam gives voice to some of his frustration noting that, when he first started on the project, Gary Kurtz and George Lucas were on-site in England and Africa, and that there was poor communication. "So we were kind of working in the dark for a while. I spent about four or five months doing animated explosions which were conceivably going to be in the film and were not."[26] They ended up using real pyrotechnic explosions, filmed from below at a fast frame rate, so they appeared to be in zero gravity. These were composited over the footage. Adam's fairly level, mature tone in the interview masks the level of frustration and disillusion that his friends remember him expressing at the time.

A number of the tests that Adam created of explosions survive among his numerous film elements. At the time he made them they were shown in-house and in the community. George Lockwood remembers seeing these. "Lucas was into this realistic-looking—his idea was this sterile future thing but everything's dirty—gritty realism to sterile future. Not the Adam abstract colorful thing. It didn't go together."[27]

Kuran, who was working in Adam's department, pointed out to him that *This Island Earth* had used real explosions for their effects and perhaps *Star Wars* should take the same approach. They had a shot of a TIE fighter breaking apart, and they needed an explosion to add to it and looked to animation for that effect. Kuran recalled that Adam animated the explosion, and it was a good animation, but it looked animated.[28]

Of course, real explosions, created through pyrotechnics, would not be an animation department's task, and, if used, the explosions would be taken away from Adam. Kuran remembers that Lucas returned from England and came to the studio practically straight from the plane to take a look at the animated explosions. Lucas had also seen and was thinking of *This Island Earth*, and Kuran recalls that he was astonished when the next day the original dailies of the explosion shots from *This Island Earth* appeared for the crew to study.

As Adam had feared, a new unit was set up to shoot real explosions, and his months of experiments and intense focus didn't make the cut. Purportedly, he felt this as a rejection, a deep failure on his part, and a lack of acknowledgment of his potential. Instead of doing something important and challenging, he was left to run the department and keep everything organized. Adam optimistically noted in the *Cinefantastique* interview that his role as department head gave him valuable experience in leading and organizing a team. And the work his team did was critical to the success of the film, from laser beams to the numerous mattes.

In this inaugural *Star Wars* movie, laser beams were not only vital to the narrative but also useful in solving some of the technical issues that arose inevitably. Edlund described a scene of the trench in the Death Star, first viewed from a distance to establish what and where it was before the camera flies into the area and down into the trench. They shot this on the Dykstraflex camera track. He explained, "All the trench shots were composites of multiple passes over the trench, because I could only get about twenty frames in one pass, and then I had to join the beginning of one pass with the end of the next pass." There were several background paintings that had various vanishing points to fit into the shot. Those, too, had to match. Edlund laughed, remembering, "... if it didn't work perfectly, then we'd add a laser!"[29] The flash of the laser beam would attract the eye and hence disguise any jumps or misalignments.

Adam contributed a number of effects, although none that could be described as "Adam animations." The multilayer-pass approach that he had taken to such an extreme in his own work was critical to the film, as Jon Seay confirms.

> ... the stuff that he came up with was the multilayering stuff and just ways of doing things, it made a big difference.... Really he came up with all the multi-pass stuff that we did on *Star Wars*. That was all Adam, because that was what he was all about. We didn't do as much as he would in his personal projects, but there was like layer after layer after layer of this stuff. So, each laser beam that was fired from the ship was... like six elements or something. I mean there were glows, there were inner cores... It was multi-pass stuff. And that was back in the day when it was all on film and if you screwed up one pass you did the whole thing over again.[30]

The primary segments that Adam created are the two large laser beam shots from the Death Star, and the delightfully animated segment near the film's beginning, where the smaller robot or "droid," R2-D2, gets zapped by the Jawas. The large laser beam that the department worked on grew to mythic proportions, as Adam insisted that it needed to be drawn large in order to work as a perfect laser beam and hold up under the high-contrast compositing process developed to add it to the movie.

Dave Berry recalls Adam's approach to one of the large laser beam shots:

> He had figured out the most complicated, obscure method of doing these laser beams for *Star Wars* that was just insane... First off, he decided that laser beams were really perfect. The light was perfect. So, the only way you can make the laser beam be really perfect was he had to draw them really big.... And his idea was to take those into a camera service and reduce them down and then put these in, just flop them into reveal mattes for them. And it made actually no difference. You could draw an ink line with a ruler and do this and you couldn't tell the difference. And then he had this really complicated method of putting this detail in them that involved shooting a core on Double-X negative—which nobody ever uses Double-X negative film—on an animation camera. And then processing that, like pushing it, or... he had this... processing technique that he wanted. And then we would bi-pack that... and do all this crazy stuff to shoot the laser beams.[31]

The light table he had for the department was sixteen feet long, as seen on the behind-the-scenes movie documentation that Berry captured. Diana Wilson, who worked on the laser beams (for the first three films), confirms the approach was extreme. Adam had ordered a special glass, a sort of milk glass, from Belgium for them to work on, and the drawings were about twelve feet long. And he had acquired an incredibly long ruler. She, too, remembers that these lasers had to be perfect and after she had drawn the line he would look at it under a loupe. It seemed extreme, especially as what they were creating was for mattes.[32]

The one shot, according to Berry, that gets closest to profiting from Adam's approach and was remotely challenging for him is an animated beam that shoots through the interior of the Death Star before an exterior shot of the beam destroying a planet. Jon Seay remembers working on that sequence and acknowledges Adam's input, noting that it was only about 96 frames, approximately 4 seconds long, but it was a huge series of loops (Figure 8.6). Byron Werner also worked on this, and he describes the drama of creating the laser beam:

> ... it's where the giant, mongo laser beam shoots down the tunnel before blasting away the planet Alderaan. Before the five or six beams meet outside and form the one big beam there's an interior shot. There's this

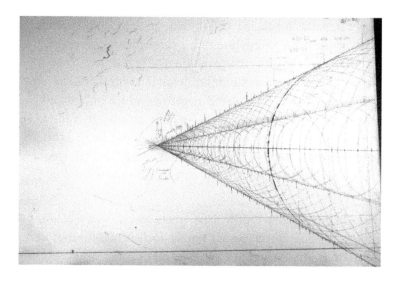

FIGURE 8.6 Adam's drawing for the laser tunnel shot referred to as 880-21. (Courtesy of LUCASFILM LTD. LLC, *Star Wars*© & TM Lucasfilm Ltd. LLC.)

enormous laser beam that's going down and, you know, Adam typically put way more detail in it than was actually needed or wanted. The beam is made up of about four or five cores and they're all moving in different directions and each has a big plasma ball that shoots down the middle of it and there were so many cells stacked up for the filming of this shot that we had to take the glass plate off of the camera and kind of put it on top and then just kind of lean on it and hit the switch and take the frame that way. I was in charge of the matte so I had to—and I painted these things and I thinned down the paint very thin and then did like four or five layers just to keep it as thin as possible, because just the paint piling up was becoming a problem. So this is this monster shot and it seemed to really consume him. And he wanted this to be his big shot I think. And it got gloriously out of control. I mean way more detail than the filmgoer will ever see. But, it was a noble undertaking.[33]

The detail would have been hard to see, especially as it had to be processed and rephotographed in the optical unit to be added to the film. A constant concern was making the black of the backgrounds opaque enough, so that light wouldn't come through and impact the shot or not fit in. These were shot on color print film and then composited in; subtleties did not hold up. This process was a frustration noted by Kuran and undoubtedly felt by Adam, who worked for perfection and had a vision of what he thought these should look like, including details.

Another incident that illustrates the types of situations that would arise in production and that weren't resolved for Adam involves the sequence that occurred *after* the laser shot in the interior of the Death Star. This scene was a memorable one owing to the drama of the narrative; Princess Leia's home planet is being destroyed. The visual and emotional impact of seeing this planet explode was not lost on Adam. He wanted it to be special, and he wanted it to be his. As Berry recounts:

> ... there's this beam that comes out of the Death Star, and explodes a planet... and Mike Ross did this really great beautiful thing and Adam got it in his mind that he could do one better. And he got into this big scene when Lucas was there telling him it had to be something special. And poor Mike Ross is sitting there—you know how it is if you're an animator and you've worked on something for months and months and then somebody says it's not any good. ... Adam did his own version of that which was also really good but they ended up using Mike Ross.[34]

Adam was able to hand-draw the animation on one scene that he was happy with; however, it did not take advantage of his signature, complex multipass process. He created the electrical current around R2-D2, or "Artoo," as he was getting ion blasted by the Jawas (Figure 8.7), and referred to this as one his "pet shots." He credited Josh Meador's animation of the Id monster in *Forbidden Planet* as his inspiration and "standard of quality."[35] Diana Wilson assisted by drawing numerous in-betweens for that animation.[36]

Adam squirreled away some of these tests, bringing them home to keep. On this film, we see the scratchy lines drawn on black around a rotoscoped outline of the short droid. He also kept some of the numerous explosion tests that were done. These now reside among his many film elements stored at the Academy Film Archive in Hollywood.

Star Wars was released in theaters on May 25, 1977, and was immediately recognized by fans, and a few critics, as a groundbreaking film. (It was rereleased in 1981 as *Star Wars IV: A New Hope.*) Adam must have felt the pressure, competition, frustration, and, also, the camaraderie, which gave birth to this project. His interview as one of the major contributors to film, in *Cinefantastique*, is three pages in length and doesn't reflect an inflated ego or manipulation of facts. He credits his team members and emphasizes that Kuran is "quite a phenomenon."[37] The captions he supplies for the

FIGURE 8.7   Adam's animation of R2-D2 being demobilized by the ion blaster. Note the VistaVision format of the film. (Courtesy of LUCASFILM LTD. LLC, *Star Wars*© & TM Lucasfilm Ltd. LLC.)

images of his department reflect his humor and somewhat irreverent perspective. What followed was a period of celebrity recognition by the swell of fans that the success of *Star Wars* attracted and of disappointment as life after *Star Wars* began.

BIBLIOGRAPHY

Los Angeles Film Forum. "Diana Wilson," "Alternate Projections: Experimental Film in Los Angeles, 1945–1980." Interviewed by Mark Toscano, oral history recorded: May 1, 2010. https://www.alternativeprojections.com/oral-histories/diana-wilson/.

Mandell, Paul. 1978. "Adam Beckett: Animation and Rotoscope Design," interview of Adam Beckett, *Cinefantastique*, Double Issue Vol.6(4)/Vol 7(1), dedicated to *Star Wars*.

Rosenfield, Paul. "40-Year-Old George Lucas Interview Predicts 'Star Wars' Future with Disney," *Los Angeles Times*, June 5, 1977. http://www.latimes.com/entertainment/herocomplex/la-et-hc-flashback-george-lucas-making-star-wars-20151206-story.html.

Sporn, Michael. "Everybody Repost," *Splog* (blog), June 25, 2012. http://www.michaelspornanimation.com/splog/?p=3050.

ENDNOTES

[1] Kathy Rose, interview by the author, March 18, 2004.

[2] Canyon Cinema's record sheet for Adam's rentals from August 1976 through December of 1983. Copies generously provided by Dominic Angerame, former executive director at Canyon Cinema.

[3] Michael Sporn, "Everybody Repost," *Splog* (blog), June 25, 2012. http://www.michaelspornanimation.com/splog/?p=3050.

[4] Pat O'Neill, interview by the author, July 26, 2003.

[5] Dave Berry, interview by the author, February 11, 2003.

[6] Richard W. Taylor II, in discussion with the author (phone), October 4, 2006.

[7] George Lockwood, in discussion with the author, (phone), October 12, 2005.

[8] Adam Beckett, typed proposal to CalArts, unspecified recipient, dated November 3, 1975. Private, Beckett's art and papers.

[9] Ric Stafford, discussion with author (phone), June 14, 2010.

[10] Taylor, Ibid.

[11] Ibid.

[12] Richard Edlund, interview by the author with Larry Cuba, March 16, 2005.

[13] Paul Rosenfield, "Lucas: Film-Maker with the Force" interview of George Lucas, *Los Angeles Times*, June 5, 1977. Current access title: "40-Year-Old George Lucas Interview Predicts 'Star Wars" Future with Disney," on *Los Angeles Times* "From the Archives." http://www.latimes.com/entertainment/herocomplex/la-et-hc-flashback-george-lucas-making-star-wars-20151206-story.html

[14] Tom Barron, in discussion with the author, (phone), August 24, 2004.

[15] Robert Blalack, email to author, March 7, 2006.

[16] Edlund, Ibid.

[17] Ibid.

[18] Blalack, Ibid.

[19] Edlund, Ibid.

[20] Paul Mandell, "Making Star Wars: Interviews by Paul Mandell/Adam Beckett, Animation and Rotoscope Design," interview of Adam Beckett, *Cinefantastique*, Double Issue Vol. 6 No. 4/Vol. 7 No. 1, dedicated to *Star Wars*, 1978, 19–21.

[21] Byron Werner, in discussion with the author, (phone), June 21, 2006.

[22] Chris Casady, in discussion with the author, (phone), February 5, 2003.

[23] Mandell, 19.

[24] Ibid., 20–21.

[25] Lockwood, Ibid.

[26] Mandell, 21.

[27] Lockwood, Ibid.

[28] Peter Kuran, discussion with the author (phone), July 23, 2004.

[29] Edlund, Ibid.

[30] Jonathan Seay, in discussion with the author (phone), April 24, 2007.

[31] Berry, Ibid.

[32] Diana Wilson, interview by the author, March 17, 2005.

[33] Werner, Ibid.

[34] Berry, Ibid.

[35] Mandell, Ibid., 20.

[36] Diana Wilson, "Diana Wilson" Interviewed by Mark Toscano. Oral History Recorded: May 1, 2010. https://www.alternativeprojections.com/oral-histories/diana-wilson/.

[37] Mandell, Ibid., 20.

CHAPTER 9

A Star Adrift

W HEN *STAR WARS* WAS first released in 1977, it was greeted with mixed reviews and long lines waiting to buy a ticket to see it. Critics, such as Roger Ebert, loved it immediately, responding to the "swashbuckling" battles and the narrative of the mythical journey.[1] A number of other critics were far less enthusiastic, finding that the movie was entertaining but lacking depth of content or character. John Simon, in *New York Magazine,* wrote a scathing review, ending with "*Star Wars* will do very nicely for those lucky enough to be children or those unlucky enough never to have grown up..."[2]

Science fiction conventions embraced the movie, the actors, and the magicians who made it possible. Adam and his colleagues were assaulted for autographs. There is a home movie filmed by Dave Berry of Adam, Doug Barnett, Robert Blalack, Chris Casady, Evan Gallas (Adam's younger half-brother), and Liz Ziegler in the desert "somewhere west of Tucson," monkeying around and shooting pistols. Adam is wearing a button that says, "May the Force Be With You" (Figure 9.1). Chris Casady took photographs during the same trip. In these images, they all look incredibly young, underscoring the fact that many who contributed to the innovative effects of this movie were barely out of college. The group

FIGURE 9.1   Photograph of Adam with *Star Wars* button, somewhere west of Tucson. (Used with permission from Chris Casady.)

was returning from the 1977 Science Fiction, Horror & Fantasy World Exposition that was held June 2 through 5 in Tucson, barely a week after the theatrical opening of *Star Wars*; most of the other attendees had yet to see the movie. A poster advertising the convention is in Adam's materials, as well as a collection of autographs he obtained there that includes the inscriptions of Harlan Ellison, Johnny Weissmuller, Friz Freleng, Robert Heinlein, and Roger Zelazny, who dated his autograph "6/4/77."

Here is where we find Adam after *Star Wars*, riding a wave of success and perhaps feeling lost after the high point of working with a team of colleagues and being the head of an important department on a groundbreaking movie. This period of his life and work leaves many questions, as he navigates his next steps, not leaving a consistent path of intention.

The inaugural Industrial Light and Magic (ILM) crew disbanded and was absorbed into various projects. Trumbull hired talent, including Jon Seay and Dave Berry, at his Future General studio to work on the final stages of *Close Encounters of the Third Kind* (December 1977). *BattleStar Galactica* (the movie) recruited John Dykstra, Peter Kuran, Richard Edlund, Jon Erland, Dave Berry, Jon Seay, and Dennis Muren. Robert Abel and Associates was working on the effects for *Star Trek: The Motion Picture* and brought Adam back to their studio.

Adam undoubtedly wanted to be at Abel's studio, to work on that project and to have access to the equipment. However, his second stint at Abel's was fairly short. Abel lost the *Star Trek* project in February of 1979, and, consequently, many on the team were let go. The task of creating the missing special and visual effects was transferred to Trumbull at Future General. That team included Jon Seay and former CalArts classmates Lisze Bechtold, Deena Burkett, and Sari Gennis. Work was parceled out to numerous other studios, including Dykstra's newly formed Apogee studio.

Adam was let go by Robert Abel and Associates several months before the studio lost the *Star Trek* project. In response, Adam posted an advertisement in *Variety* that said "Dear BOB Abel, 'I don't GET it?!' LOVE, Adam Beckett." The ad appeared sometime just before July 14, 1978. The content was puzzling and also alarmingly public. Variety is an important trade paper and would have been seen by everyone working in the Hollywood movie industry. Friends remember cringing when the ad came out, wondering at Adam's motivation and judgment in doing this; he was burning bridges, whether he meant to or not.

The ad included a stylized self-portrait and a distorted triangle with an eye, similar to the pyramid found on his Canyon Cinema promotional page and on U.S. paper currency. The symbol is the "Eye of Providence" and refers to the all-seeing vision of the Christian God. Adam has inscribed the letters "I.C.U." at the base of his triangle. Under his name, he wrote "STAR WARZ ALUMNUS ASSOC." In an odd gesture, he has written "Give $ to the California Institute of the Art" in text that winds around the edge of the ad, ending with "Yay Cal Arts" at the top, albeit upside down. As he did on his Canyon Cinema page, he has rubber-stamped "SECURITY INFORMATION," "SECRET," and "CONFIDENTIAL."

Those who knew him often cite *Star Wars* as a turning point for Adam, as he became more unpredictable; however, there are conflicting stories. When asked how he recalls Adam, Richard Taylor thought that, on his return to Abel's studio, Adam had grown professionally, in that he was better at working with clients and realizing that efficiency mattered.[3] Other sources remember him acting out as if to get attention from Abel and wondered if his behavior was due to drugs or alcohol or fallout after *Star Wars*.

On April 3, 1978, the Academy of Motion Picture Arts and Sciences presented the award for best visual effects to the Industrial Light and Magic team for their work on *Star Wars*; the Oscar went to John Dykstra, Richard Edlund, Robert Blalack, John Stears, and Grant McCune. Adam was conspicuously absent from the list. With the critical role that his department played in this movie of illusions, Adam's omission had to have negatively impacted him. Later that year, Lucas decided to relocate ILM's studio north to Marin County, closer to his home base, to start production on the next *Star Wars, The Empire Strikes Back*. Adam's ILM/CalArt's colleagues Dave Berry, Chris Casady, Peter Kuran, and Diana Wilson would work on that film, joined by Loring Doyle, who followed his classmates' path from CalArts to the industry. Kuran was hired to head the rotoscoping and animation area. Adam was not asked to join them. (In a somewhat ironic note, Lucas sold LucasFilms and the *Star Wars* franchise to Disney in 2012; members of his initial effects crew came from the school that Disney had built.)

Adam had changed as he entered the industry and now had been changed *by* the industry. In addition to studio politics and fierce competition, the industry had introduced Adam to cocaine. Doyle recalls that, just a couple of years ago, while they were still students, Adam had advised against drugs, saying that they weren't needed for creativity.[4] The industry demanded more than creativity; it required long hours and almost manic drive. Adam had worked long hours, notoriously and obsessively, while he was a student, but back then, he was driven by his passion for his independent vision. If indeed Adam was using cocaine, it would account for some of the changes that people noticed. What had been confidence now appeared as an inflated ego. His behavior became erratic, with moments of paranoia. His visits to CalArt's campus were halted after *Star Wars* owing to his behavior and to changes in personnel on campus. Times were changing. There are numerous rumors from this time; most have grown through reputation and many were dramatized at the time, perhaps in an effort to put a halt to Adam being on campus. His behavior may have been intimidating, and he may have been acting out more, but those who were around him at that time concur that he was not dangerous.

Kuran keenly observed that when a project as immense as *Star Wars* "comes too early in your life you may... get mixed emotions about the rest of your life. ... film business in general isn't necessarily a great business to grow culturally and spiritually in... or continuously."[5] Jon Seay's perspective was that Adam's experience on *Star Wars* was a disappointment, and after it, Adam had "had it." He explained, "Hollywood is not really for the free spirit kind of guy, unless you're in control. It's a business; it's all about making money. They like people they can tell what to do. Adam wasn't one of those guys."[6]

What many people were not aware of is that Adam's father had died suddenly, tragically, and mysteriously, in a fall from his apartment window in September of 1977, 4 months after the release of *Star Wars*. While his father was described as eccentric and was a chronic alcoholic, Adam had maintained a relationship with him and endeavored to win his approval, which was difficult to obtain. William Beckett had visited his son at the industrial studio, as they worked on *Star Wars,* and rather than being impressed, he was critical of the messy state of the studio.[7] However, according to his mother, at the time his father died, the two had not spoken in months owing to a dispute. His father's death had a devastating emotional impact on Adam and was the catalyst for a downward spiral.

Kuran's studio, Visual Concept Entertainment (VCE), was doing work for a Roger Korman movie, *Piranha*, released in August of 1978. Casady was working with Kuran, and he and O'Neill contributed to the effects for the film. After Adam was released from Abel's, Kuran recruited him to animate a scene of a swarm of the attacking fish. He then asked Adam to join him on *The Day Time Ended,* directed by John "Bud" Carlos. He was unable to get a commitment from Adam. *Piranha* was the last known commercial film that Adam would work on.

Adam had completed six independent films between the years 1972 and 1975. His prolific output was interrupted by the commercial work that he began when he entered Abel's studio. (In the *Cinefantastique* article, Adam cites his professional work as the reason why he halted his graduate studies.) He continued to draw and show in-progress versions of *Life in the Atom* and *Knotte Grosse*. His past accomplishments and the continued distribution of his work sustained his renown as an independent animator.

In February 1977, as Adam turned 27 years and was working at ILM on *Star Wars, Millimeter* magazine published a special animation issue that included the brief article "Poets of the Single Frame: Young American Animators," by Thelma Schenkel, attesting to the rising force of independent animation. She singled out 10 rising stars: Eliot Noyes, Jr., George Griffin, Kathy Rose, Al Jarnow, Dennis Pies (now working as Sky David), Mary Beams, Adam Beckett, Richard Protovin, Kathleen Laughlin, and Maureen Selwood. These animators were not working in the tradition of comics or story illustration, as she pointed out, but in a more "poetic" mode. Referencing Adam's observation from the 1974 interview with Russett, she writes that "Adam Beckett... feels that 'we are at the beginning of a wonderful golden age of animation'; his innovative, unconventional films will have a lot to do with making it happen."[8]

In late 1978, Adam rejoined his independent animation community, at least in print, in *Frames: A Selection of Drawings and Statements by Independent American Animators.* That publication was a who's who of 1970s American animation, instigated by a collection of animators in New York City, who gathered to discuss the work that they were making and to share connections and opportunities. The call for submissions explained that they were creating a book that would illustrate the "diversity of personal, experimental animated film"; it was signed by George Griffin, Victor Faccinto, Al Jarnow, Kathy Rose, and Anita Thacher. The compiled submissions provide invaluable and fascinating documentation of the creative diversity within the independent community at that particular period of time.[9]

Seventy artists (counting Frank and Caroline Mouris as two artists, although they contributed one entry) were represented. The pages that they submitted were varied, demonstrating the broad range of individual approaches to animation. There were images, with text discussing individual processes or ideas about animation (Ken Brown), sequences of wonderful drawings used in animation (Paul Glabicki), or pieces made specifically for the book such as Linda Heller's "INSTANTMOVIE" with "everything you need for an animated movie." Peter Rose and Pat O'Neill were included, even though they were more often referenced as experimental filmmakers. Their inclusion speaks to the broad definition that this community applied to animation. All 10 of Schenkel's emerging new "poets" were included in *Frames* alongside established artists such as James Whitney, Stan VanDerBeek, Robert Breer, and Jules Engel.

Adam's page does not reference his animations or the topic of making animation. Rather, it is a missive to his fellow animators and provides insight into Adam's personality during early 1978. His tone is jovial, but the material he submitted is all about him, not his art. The content is consistent with his earlier doodles that often contained written thoughts and proclamations. He filled the page with six self-declared aphorisms, with one stating that his political theory was absolute anarchy and warning that it was dangerous to annoy fellow anarchists, as "some of us have the H-Bomb." He was being light-hearted, but there is a hint of cynicism. His exuberant nature filled the page, yet he had missed an opportunity to promote and share his animation. At the top of his page, there is a detailed crosshatched "HI K.R."—his wave to Rose. There is a quote, "We dance at the edge of a great incandescent explosion," echoing language from Orson Welles's 1938 "War of the Worlds" radio program. At the bottom, he signed off with "I LOVE YOU brothers & SISTERS by Adam K. Beckett" (Figure 9.2).

Adam was caught between his independent work and the industry, trying to find a way to resolve the two. Schenkel, in her article on the "poets," reported that Adam was "currently trying to combine work on *Life in the Atom* (which he has been working on for seven years), a new version of *Dear Janice*, and *Knotte Grosse* with his commercial work."[10] In order to do any work, personal or commercial, he needed equipment. He obtained a camera through Dan McLaughlin at University of California, Los Angeles

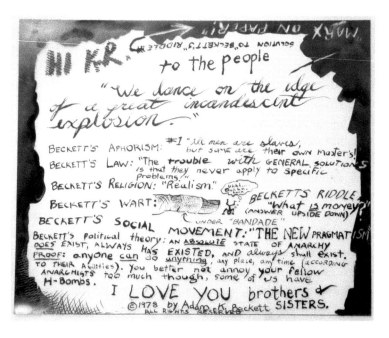

FIGURE 9.2   Adam's film positive for his page in *Frames*, 1978. (Used with permission from Beckett's family.)

and spoke of a "secret" studio in Hollywood—which could have alluded to work that he was doing at Abel's or another place he hoped to secure. No studio was ever found; his mountains of drawings and his animation setup were in his house.

The awkward position that Adam was in reflects independent animation's uncertain path at that point in time as well. There was a push and pull between cartoons, independent animation, experimental film, auteur film, video, and Hollywood movies (which were increasingly using visual effects). Youngblood's vision of expanded cinema was taking place as media technologies mushroomed and artists, alongside commercial studios, explored new forms of content.

Perhaps, more backward looking than forward, the National Endowment for the Arts launched a pilot program called Short Films Showcase. The premise was to have short films made by independent filmmakers, distributed theatrically to play before the "proper feature films," harkening back to times when theater goers could "see a little travelogue and cartoon and previews and then the movie."[11] Reportedly, it was the idea of director Robert Wise, who hoped to introduce these artists, and the short form, to the public and make them more aware of "the development and innovation which has occurred in this art form in recent years." Martin Scorsese and Francis Ford Coppola were on the panel that selected the films. Announced in late 1978, the 6 inaugural films were *Clay* by Eliot Noyes, Jr., *Frank Film* by Frank Mouris, *Lapis* by James Whitney, *Evolution of the Red Star* by Adam Beckett, *Light* by Jordan Belson, and *Gulls and Buoys* by Robert Breer. Adam was in good company. Each filmmaker received $3000 for distribution rights.

While described as "short films," these are all animated; however, they are nothing like the cartoons of earlier times. The program did not succeed, and there is barely a record of it. This may have been an issue of logistics in overseeing and managing the program, as much as it was the result of audience response. It was a long shot, trying to create symbiosis between

Hollywood movies and the independent work of animation artists. This would become even more of a stretch with the advent of the "blockbuster" movie, initiated by *Jaws* in the summer of 1975, and made a permanent fixture by *Star Wars* in May of 1977.

Animation by Adam and a number of his peers such as Sky David (then Dennis Pies), Sara Petty, Larry Cuba, and Chris Casady are abstractions and align more with avant-garde and experimental films, such as the work of Oskar Fischinger, Stan Brakhage, and Jordan Belson and even the assemblage-like open narratives of Pat O'Neill. Even so, the animated form was excluded from theoretical discussions around cinema, being relegated to a less serious moving art form. Yet, the newer technology of video *was* being considered in critical forums. The neglect of animation slowly began to change in the late 1980s. In 1987, the Society of Animation Studies was founded by Harvey Deneroff in response to the lack of inclusion in film or arts scholarship. They held their first conference in 1989 at the Animation Workshop at UCLA, which was headed by Dan McLaughlin.

Adam's animated work was situated at the crossroads of emerging video image processing and computer graphics and in dialog with those forms, using his own language and technical finesse. After his experience in the industry, he wanted to continue his independent work but had lost direction. Following the careers of his peers and the other "poets" of animation, we see the paths that people found or created for themselves. Dave Berry worked with ILM until 1984 and won an Academy Award for Best Visual Effects in 1985 for his work on *Cocoon*. At the time of this writing, he is still making his own work and staying abreast of digital technology. Chris Casady continued working on visual effects projects, eventually running his own solo studio. He has won two Clio awards for animation in commercials and is currently creating independent work that appears in festivals. Larry Cuba went on to work independently and made three award-winning abstract computer-animated films: *3/78, Two Space,* and *Calculated Movements.* He continues to work in the development of the programmed moving image. Sky David has balanced making art, as Sky David Studio, and is working as a physical therapist and molecular biologist, through Sky David Lymphatics. Caroline Leaf animated for the National Film Board of Canada and now works from her studio in London, animating and painting. Deanna Morse joined the faculty at Grand Valley State in Michigan in 1979, where she taught for more than 30 years. She's made numerous animations and continues an active studio practice. Kathy Rose reunited her visual work with her dance and performance background to create unique moving-image performances that delve into mythical entities and experience, inspired by Japanese theater and art. She has taught at the University of the Arts for many years. Rose received a Guggenheim Fellowship in 2003. One can only surmise what direction Adam may have taken, had he been able to continue.

In late 1978 and early 1979, Adam grew more reclusive. There are a few drawings dated 1978, but little is known about what he was working on. On March 6, 1979, he was asleep in his bathtub, when the lamp on his animation table caught fire. Tragically, Adam did not wake up. In an eerie and incomprehensibly horrific coincidence, his sister Morgan was murdered earlier the same morning, in Olympia, Washington. Owing to the timing, it is unlikely that he knew about her death.

The following day, after the fire was extinguished, friends gathered at the site, stunned. The wind was blowing papers that had been rescued from his house across the yard. O'Neill recalls that the largest ball of film tape he'd ever seen was still smoldering on the porch. Mark Whitney was reunited with a letter that he had sent to Adam, years earlier, among the papers that were tumbling around them.[12] As Whitney so gracefully expressed, Adam was an authentic being and his artwork was—and remains—a vestige of his navigating and negotiating through a complex life.

Friends joined Adam's sister, Deirdre, in an effort to collect his work, with the intent to organize and preserve it. Materials were scavenged from all sources. These were moved to a vault space, provided by the Whitney family. A detailed inventory of film elements was recorded, which filled 30 legal-size pages, with 956 itemized individual elements. It makes apparent the incredible number of elements used to create a single film and how much work Adam created. There were a few release prints, but the bulk of the materials included mattes and wedges, tests, loops, a few home movies, experiments from his work on *Star Wars,* and elements from the works in progress, *Knotte Grosse* and *Life in the Atom.*

This inventory offered critical insight and guidance more than 20 years later, when the iotaCenter acquired the films through a deed of gift by Adam's mother, Julie. The iotaCenter is a nonprofit in Los Angeles that is committed to abstraction and experimental work in animation, video, and film. Its founder, Larry Cuba, and founding board members Sara Petty and Roberta Friedman, were Adam's friends and colleagues. The boxes of film elements were delivered to the Academy of Motion Picture Arts and Sciences' film archive, where Mark Toscano, with interns from iotaCenter, inventoried and examined them. Rebecca Newman, then with the iotaCenter, wrote grant proposals to the National Film Preservation Foundation that were successful in securing funding to restore Adam's films. Toscano began the arduous task of finding and piecing together the best surviving elements to work with, as he began their restoration.[13] It wasn't a straightforward process, as there were many pieces, and, as Toscano pointed out, Adam basically was "using the rules as a launching point."

More than 31 years after the Oscar was awarded to colleagues on the visual effects team, Adam was recognized by the Academy of Motion Picture Arts and Sciences' Science and Technology Council. On the evening of August 17, 2009, "Infinite Animation: The Work of Adam Beckett," was held at the Linwood Dunn Theater in Hollywood to pay tribute to Adam Beckett. Colleagues and fans gathered to see his restored films and to learn more about his work through a presentation and panel discussion. A stereographic image of Adam (taken by Casady) filled the screen, and his many loops were projected in an amazingly choreographed process led by Mark Toscano, with animator Jodie Mack and others relaying loops to the projectors, as people entered the theater. Colleagues, classmates, fans, and family came out to celebrate Adam. The event was sold out. Cohosted by Richard Win Taylor II, his friend and colleague from Abel's studio, and me, his biographer, the night featured screenings of Adam's work and a panel discussion that filled the stage with colleagues and friends: Beth Block, Dave Berry, Richard Edlund, Roberta Friedman, Chris Casady, Pat O'Neill, and David Wilson.

It is important to note that Adam "was well loved," as David Wilson made sure to express when introducing Adam's work in "Optic Antics," a screening of early optical printing films by CalArts students at the Museum of Modern Art.[14] This was evidenced in the spirit of the Academy event and the tremendous turnout. Adam's presence at CalArts remains mythical, with tales of his large personality and spirit persisting even today. His legacy continues through the screening of his work and in the fascination that the infinitely animating cycle still inspires in emerging animators. His life and work were extraordinary, filled with quirks, idiosyncrasies, and extremes. While he exited too young, he left a persistent trail of innovation in animation and effects, through his influence on those whose life and work he touched and in the fantastic films that continue to take viewers on transformative journeys of sight and sound.

BIBLIOGRAPHY

Ebert, Roger. "Star Wars," Reviews, Roger Ebert.com. Blog. https://www.rogerebert.com/reviews/star-wars-1977.

Griffin, George. 1978. *FRAMES: A Selection of Drawings and Statements by Independent American Animators.* Montpelier, Vermont: Capital City Press. (Not in print.)

Lincoln, Kevin and John Simon. "Looking Back at New York's Critical 1977 Review of *Star Wars,*" *The Vulture* (New York Magazine), December 12, 2017. http://www.vulture.com/2015/12/nymag-original-star-wars-review-1977.html.

Schenkel, Thelma. 1977. "Poets of the Single Frame: Young American," *Millimeter Magazine.* http://www.michaelspornanimation.com/splog/?p=1670.

Toscano, Mark. "Five Films by Adam Beckett (1973–75)/FIFTEEN YEARS? Part 4: 2006," *Preservation Insanity,* blog, 2018. https://preservationinsanity.wordpress.com/2018/06/30/five-films-by-adam-beckett-1973-75-fifteen-years-part-4-2006/.

The Daily Courier. "The Short Movies," *The Daily Courier* (Connellsville, Pennsylvania), December 29, 1977, 16. Newpapers.com, retrieved February 9, 2017.

ENDNOTES

1. Roger Ebert, https://www.rogerebert.com/reviews/star-wars-1977.

2. Kevin Lincoln and John Simon, "Looking Back at New York's Critical 1977 Review of *Star Wars,*" *The Vulture,* (New York Magazine), December 12, 2017. http://www.vulture.com/2015/12/nymag-original-star-wars-review-1977.html.

3. Richard W. Taylor, II, in discussion with the author (phone), October 4, 2006.

4. Loring Doyle, in discussion with the author (phone), January 28, 2007.

5. Peter Kuran, in discussion with the author (phone), July 3, 2004.

6. Jonathan Seay, in discussion with the author, April 24, 2007.

7. Chris Casady, in discussion with the author, February 5, 2003.

8. Thelma (Talia) Schenkel, "Poets of the Single Frame: Young American," *Millimeter Magazine,* 1977, 69. http://www.michaelspornanimation.com/splog/?p=1670.

9. George Griffin, (assembled by), *FRAMES: A Selection of Drawings and Statements by Independent American Animators,* 1978. Not in print. Capital City Press, Montpelier, Vermont.

10. Schenkel, Ibid.

11. The Daily Courier. "The Short Movies," *The Daily Courier* (Connellsville, Pennsylvania), December 29, 1977, 16. Newpapers.com, retrieved February 9, 2017.

[12] Mark Whitney, interview by the author with Larry Cuba, April 12, 2003.

[13] Mark Toscano, "Five Films by Adam Beckett (1973–75) / FIFTEEN YEARS? Part 4: 2006," *Preservation Insanity*, blog, June 30, 2018. https://preservationinsanity.wordpress.com/2018/06/30/five-films-by-adam-beckett-1973-75-fifteen-years-part-4-2006/.

[14] David Wilson, introducing Adam's work at "Optic Antics," program included in series "*TOMORROWLAND*: CalArts in Moving Pictures," August 5, 2006. Museum of Modern Art, New York. Curated by Joshua Siegel.

Index